CAST-IRON BAKING

SCRATCH RECIPES FOR YOUR FAVORITE SKILLET

BROOKE BELL

83
PRESS

83 Press
1900 International Park Drive, Suite 50
Birmingham, Alabama 35243
www.83press.com

ISBN #9781940772431
Printed in China

OATMEAL-TOFFEE COOKIE
PAGE 110

CONTENTS

INTRODUCTION

Baking is an expression of love, especially when batter is poured into cast-iron skillets that have been passed down through generations and layered with decades of memories. When you cook for loved ones, you nourish and satisfy—but when you bake, you extend a warm hug to family and friends.

I come from a family of bakers. My grandmother owned every shape of cake pan there was, and her kitchen cabinets were filled with baking tools. She spent years crafting beautiful cakes for holidays and special occasions. My mother carries on the tradition and bakes a cream cheese pound cake that's so perfect—crisp edges with a slightly undercooked ribbon in the center—it makes me homesick just thinking about it. This cookbook is full of the seasonal recipes that remind me of the great bakers in my life. They're rustic, humble, and full of love.

**STRAWBERRY
SKILLET CAKE**
PAGE 37

SPRING

This is the season of new beginnings—fresh herbs, colorful produce, and sweet berries abound. Get ready to bake your way through this most-delicious time of year. Springtime flavors will bring joy to your kitchen all season long.

BACON & CHIVE CORN MUFFINS

These stir-together muffins are perfect to serve alongside a bowl of soup or a vegetable plate. Plus, they're a great way to use some of the bacon grease I always have stored in my refrigerator. I don't like to waste a single drop of that "liquid gold."

MAKES 12

1　cup yellow cornmeal
1　cup all-purpose flour
1　tablespoon baking powder
1　teaspoon salt
2　large eggs, lightly beaten
1¼　cups whole milk
3　tablespoons bacon drippings
¼　cup chopped cooked bacon
2　tablespoons chopped fresh chives

Preheat oven to 425°. Spray a 12-cup cast-iron muffin pan with cooking spray. Place pan in oven to preheat for 3 to 4 minutes.

In a large bowl, whisk together cornmeal, flour, baking powder, and salt. Stir in eggs, milk, and bacon drippings just until combined; stir in bacon and chives. Spoon batter into prepared muffin cups, filling ¾ full.

Bake until golden brown, 15 to 20 minutes. Let cool in pan for 5 minutes; serve warm.

BAKING TIP

Lightly brush the muffins with melted butter while they're still warm for a richer flavor.

BUTTERMILK-RAISIN SODA BREAD

Celebrate St. Patrick's Day with this rustic soda bread. It's best served warm, right when it comes out of the oven.

½ cup plus 2 tablespoons cold butter, cubed and divided
5 cups all-purpose flour
½ cup sugar
1 tablespoon baking powder
1 teaspoon baking soda
1 teaspoon salt
1½ cups raisins
2⅓ cups whole buttermilk
1 large egg

Preheat oven to 350°. Place 2 tablespoons cold butter in a 12-inch cast-iron skillet, and place skillet in oven until butter is melted

In a large bowl, whisk together flour, sugar, baking powder, baking soda, and salt. Using a pastry blender or your fingers, cut in remaining ½ cup cold butter until mixture is crumbly; stir in raisins.

In a small bowl, whisk together buttermilk and egg. Gradually stir buttermilk mixture into flour mixture just until dry ingredients are moistened. Pour batter into prepared skillet.

Bake until golden brown, 30 to 35 minutes. Let cool in pan for 10 minutes; serve warm.

BAKING TIP

Give your buttermilk a good shake before you measure it for this recipe. If you're not a fan of raisins, you can use cranberries, blueberries, or currants instead.

CARAMEL PECAN BANANA COFFEE CAKE

With a layer of caramel sauce baked into the cake and more spooned on top, this coffee cake will remind you of the iconic New Orleans dessert, Bananas Foster.

MAKES 1 (9-INCH) CAKE

CARAMEL:
- 1½ cups sugar
- 3 tablespoons water
- ½ cup heavy whipping cream
- ¼ cup unsalted butter, softened

TOPPING:
- ⅓ cup firmly packed light brown sugar
- 3 tablespoons all-purpose flour
- ¼ teaspoon ground cinnamon
- 2 tablespoons unsalted butter, melted
- ½ cup pecans, chopped

CAKE:
- ½ cup unsalted butter, softened
- 1 cup sugar
- 2 large eggs
- 2 bananas, mashed
- ½ cup sour cream
- 1 teaspoon vanilla extract
- 1½ cups all-purpose flour
- 1 teaspoon baking powder
- ½ teaspoon kosher salt
- ½ cup pecans, chopped

FOR CARAMEL:

In a large skillet, stir together sugar and 3 tablespoons water. Cook over medium-high heat, without stirring, until mixture is amber colored, about 10 minutes. Remove from heat; stir in cream and butter. Let cool in skillet, stirring frequently.

Preheat oven to 350°. Spray a 9-inch cast-iron skillet with cooking spray.

FOR TOPPING:

In a medium bowl, whisk together brown sugar, flour, and cinnamon. With a mixer at medium speed, beat in melted butter until crumbly. Stir in pecans; set aside.

FOR CAKE:

In a large bowl, beat butter and sugar with a mixer at medium speed until fluffy, 3 to 4 minutes, stopping to scrape sides of bowl. Add eggs, one at a time, beating well after each addition. Beat in banana, sour cream, and vanilla.

In a medium bowl, whisk together flour, baking powder, and salt. Reduce mixer speed to low. Gradually add flour mixture to butter mixture, beating just until combined. Spread half of batter into prepared pan. Drizzle with ¾ cup warm caramel, and sprinkle with pecans. Top with remaining batter, and swirl in ¼ cup caramel. Sprinkle with topping.

Bake until a wooden pick inserted in center comes out clean, 45 to 50 minutes, loosely covering with foil to prevent excess browning, if necessary. Drizzle with remaining caramel.

STRAWBERRY SWIRL BREAD

Don't let this yeasted bread intimidate you...it's double-packed with strawberries and worth the extra effort.

MAKES 8 TO 10 SERVINGS

⅔ cup warm whole milk (105° to 110°)
1 tablespoon granulated sugar
1 (0.25-ounce) package active
  dry yeast
3 cups all-purpose flour, divided
¼ cup unsalted butter, melted
2 large eggs
1 teaspoon kosher salt
1 (13-ounce) jar strawberry
  preserves
½ cups fresh strawberries, chopped
1 cup confectioners' sugar
1 tablespoon heavy whipping cream

In the bowl of a stand mixer fitted with the paddle attachment, combine warm milk, granulated sugar, and yeast. Let stand until mixture is foamy, about 10 minutes. Add 1 cup flour, beating at low speed until combined. Add melted butter and ½ cup flour, beating until combined. Add eggs, beating to combine. Gradually add salt and remaining 1½ cups flour, beating until a soft dough forms.

Spray a large bowl with cooking spray. Place dough in bowl, turning to grease top. Cover and let rise in a warm, draft-free place (75°) until doubled in size, about 1 hour.

Spray a 10-inch cast-iron skillet with cooking spray.

On a lightly floured surface, roll dough into an 18x16-inch rectangle. Spread with preserves, leaving a ½-inch border. Sprinkle with strawberries. Starting with one long side, roll up dough, jelly-roll style, pressing seam to seal. Place seam side down on a cutting board, and cut in half lengthwise, pinching top to seal. Carefully twist dough pieces around each other, and place in prepared skillet, cut side up, tucking end underneath. Cover and let rise in a warm, draft-free place (75°) until doubled in size, about 45 minutes.

Preheat oven to 350°.

Bake until a wooden pick inserted in center comes out clean, 35 to 40 minutes, loosely covering with foil to prevent excess browning, if necessary. Let cool completely.

In a small bowl, whisk together confectioners' sugar and cream until smooth. Drizzle over cooled bread.

CARROT COFFEE CAKE

Topped with tangy buttermilk whipped cream, this coffee cake is a decadent weekend breakfast treat.

TOPPING:
- ½ cup sweetened flaked coconut
- ⅓ cup pecans, chopped
- 1½ tablespoons firmly packed light brown sugar
- 1 tablespoon all-purpose flour
- 1 tablespoon unsalted butter, melted

CAKE:
- ¾ cup vegetable oil
- ½ cup firmly packed light brown sugar
- ½ cup granulated sugar
- 2 large eggs
- 1 teaspoon vanilla extract
- 1 cup all-purpose flour
- 1½ teaspoons ground cinnamon
- ½ teaspoon baking powder
- ¼ teaspoon kosher salt
- 1 cup shredded carrot
- ½ cup crushed pineapple, drained
- ½ cup pecan halves, chopped
- ½ cup sweetened flaked coconut

BUTTERMILK WHIPPED CREAM:
- 1 cup heavy whipping cream
- ½ cup whole buttermilk
- 2½ tablespoons sugar

Preheat oven to 350°. Spray a 9-inch cast-iron skillet with cooking spray.

FOR TOPPING:
In a medium bowl, stir together coconut, pecans, brown sugar, and flour. Stir in melted butter until combined; set aside.

FOR CAKE:
In a large bowl, beat oil, sugars, eggs, and vanilla with a mixer at medium speed until combined.

In a medium bowl, whisk together flour, cinnamon, baking powder, and salt. Reduce mixer speed to low. Gradually add flour mixture to oil mixture, beating just until combined. Stir in carrot, pineapple, pecans, and coconut. Spread batter into prepared skillet.

Bake for 25 minutes. Sprinkle with topping, and bake until a wooden pick inserted in center comes out clean and coconut is lightly golden, 7 to 10 minutes more.

FOR WHIPPED CREAM:
In a medium bowl, beat cream and buttermilk with a mixer at high speed until foamy. Gradually add sugar, beating until stiff peaks form. Serve with cake.

HOMEMADE DILL ROLLS

When bunches of fresh dill show up at the farmers' market, I know spring has officially arrived.
These rolls are perfect to accompany grilled lamb or glazed ham on your Easter sideboard.

MAKES 12

1   (0.25-ounce) package active dry yeast
¼   cup lukewarm water
2⅔   cups bread flour
1   large egg
1   cup small curd whole-milk cottage cheese
¼   cup chopped fresh dill
3   tablespoons sugar
1   tablespoon unsalted butter, softened
1½   teaspoons kosher salt
1½   teaspoons onion powder
½   teaspoon baking soda
½   teaspoon ground black pepper
Garnish: melted butter, sea salt

In a small bowl, stir together yeast and ¼ cup lukewarm water. Let stand until bubbly, about 5 minutes.

In the bowl of a stand mixer fitted with the dough hook attachment, combine flour, egg, cottage cheese, dill, sugar, butter, salt, onion powder, baking soda, and pepper. Add yeast mixture, and beat at medium speed until a dough forms. Reduce mixer speed to low, and beat until dough is smooth and elastic, about 10 minutes.

Spray a large bowl with cooking spray. Place dough in bowl, turning to grease top. Cover and let rise in a warm, draft-free place (75°) until doubled in size, about 1½ hours.

Lightly spray a 10-inch cast-iron skillet with cooking spray. Divide dough into 12 equal portions. Roll each piece into a ball; place in prepared skillet. Cover and let rise in a warm, draft-free place (75°) until doubled in size, about 1 hour.

Preheat oven to 325°.

Bake until golden brown, about 20 minutes. Brush rolls with melted butter, and sprinkle with sea salt, if desired.

LEMON POPPY SEED CAKE

Spring always makes me crave the lemon poppy seed muffins I made on Saturday mornings as a child—straight from the Martha White pouch. This skillet cake features the same classic flavor, made from scratch.

MAKES 1 (9-INCH) CAKE

1	cup granulated sugar
2	lemons, zested and juiced
½	cup unsalted butter, softened
2	large eggs
1⅓	cups all-purpose flour
1¼	teaspoons baking powder
¼	teaspoon kosher salt
½	cup Greek yogurt
2	tablespoons poppy seeds
2	cups confectioners' sugar

Preheat oven to 350°. Spray a 9-inch cast-iron skillet with cooking spray.

In a large bowl, beat granulated sugar and zest with a mixer at medium speed until well combined, 3 to 5 minutes. Add butter, and beat until fluffy, 3 to 4 minutes, stopping to scrape sides of bowl. Add eggs, one at a time, beating well after each addition.

In a medium bowl, whisk together flour, baking powder, and salt. Reduce mixer speed to low. Gradually add flour mixture to butter mixture alternately with yogurt, beginning and ending with flour mixture, beating just until combined after each addition. Fold in poppy seeds. Pour batter into prepared skillet.

Bake until a wooden pick inserted in center comes out clean, 30 to 35 minutes. Let cool completely.

In a small bowl, whisk together confectioners' sugar and lemon juice until smooth. Drizzle over cooled cake.

BUTTERMILK BISCUITS

Saturday mornings are made for these biscuits. Folding the dough yields tall biscuits
with lots of flaky layers, ideal for drenching with honey or cane syrup.

MAKES ABOUT 8

2 cups all-purpose flour
1 tablespoon baking powder
¾ teaspoon kosher salt
½ teaspoon sugar
½ cup cold unsalted butter, cubed
1 cup whole buttermilk, divided
1 tablespoon unsalted butter,
   melted

Preheat oven to 425°.

In a large bowl, whisk together flour, baking powder, salt, and sugar. Using
a pastry blender or your fingers, cut in cold butter until mixture is crumbly.
Gradually add ¾ cup buttermilk, stirring until dry ingredients are moistened.
Add remaining ¼ cup buttermilk, if needed.

On a lightly floured surface, gently knead dough 4 or 5 times. Roll dough to
¾-inch thickness. Fold dough in half, and roll to ¾-inch thickness. Using a
2½-inch round cutter dipped in flour, cut dough, rerolling scraps once. Place
biscuits in an 8-inch cast-iron skillet, overlapping slightly.

Bake until lightly browned, about 17 minutes. Brush with melted butter.

BISCUIT BAKING TIPS

Transfer your biscuit dough to a floured work surface. Knead the dough a few times, or just until the dough comes together. If you see some pieces of butter and a little flour in the dough, you have succeeded. Over mixing will result in a tough, dense biscuit.

Pat or gently roll your dough to ¾-inch thickness, and fold the dough in half. Folding creates layers in the dough that help leaven and ultimately produce a light and tender biscuit. Roll the dough to ¾-inch thickness again. At this point, use your floured cutter (or in a pinch, a thin-sided glass), and cut straight down to make biscuits out of the dough. You can reroll scraps once—any more than that, and you risk making a tough biscuit. And that's it—place your biscuits in a cast-iron skillet, and bake in your preheated oven until golden brown and delicious.

FRENCH TOAST CASSEROLE

Hit the day-old bread shelf at your local bakery for some good country sourdough,
and plan to serve this centerpiece warm from the oven with lots of spoons.

MAKES ABOUT 6 SERVINGS

5   tablespoons unsalted butter,
     melted and divided
1   (12-ounce) loaf day-old sourdough
     bread, cut into ½-inch-thick slices
6   large eggs
3   cups whole milk
⅓   cup plus 1 tablespoon granulated
     sugar, divided
1   teaspoon vanilla extract
¼   teaspoon kosher salt
¼   teaspoon ground cinnamon
2   cups sliced fresh strawberries
2   tablespoons confectioners' sugar

Brush a 10-inch cast-iron skillet with 1 tablespoon melted butter. Add bread to pan in a circle, overlapping slices.

In a large bowl, whisk together eggs, milk, ⅓ cup granulated sugar, vanilla, salt, and cinnamon. Pour over bread. Drizzle with remaining 4 tablespoons melted butter. Gently press bread into egg mixture. Cover and let stand for 30 minutes.

In a medium bowl, stir together strawberries and remaining 1 tablespoon granulated sugar. Let stand for 30 minutes.

Preheat oven to 350°. Uncover casserole; gently press bread into egg mixture.

Bake until puffed, golden brown, and egg mixture in center is set, about 40 minutes. Top with strawberries; sprinkle with confectioners' sugar. Serve immediately.

SAUSAGE & CHIVE BISCUIT WEDGES

These biscuit wedges are a marriage of scones and the Southern, all-time party favorite, the sausage ball.

MAKES 6

2   cups all-purpose flour
2   tablespoons chopped fresh chives
1   tablespoon baking powder
¾   teaspoon kosher salt
½   teaspoon baking soda
½   teaspoon sugar
⅔   cup cooked, crumbled, and cooled
     pork breakfast sausage
1   cup whole buttermilk, divided
⅓   cup plus 1 tablespoon unsalted
     butter, melted and divided

Preheat oven to 425°.

In a large bowl, whisk together flour, chives, baking powder, salt, baking soda, and sugar; stir in sausage.

In a small bowl, combine ¾ cup buttermilk and ⅓ cup melted butter. Make a well in center of flour mixture; add buttermilk mixture. Stir until dry ingredients are moistened, adding remaining ¼ cup buttermilk, if needed. Spoon dough into wells of a 9-inch cast-iron wedge pan, mounding dough.

Bake until lightly browned, about 17 minutes. Let cool in pan for 10 minutes. Run a knife around edges of biscuits. Remove from pan. Brush with remaining 1 tablespoon melted butter; serve warm.

BAKING TIP

If you don't own a wedge pan, bake in a
9-inch skillet and cut into wedges.

SKILLET CARROT CAKE

This recipe is a relaxed version of my mother's towering three-layer carrot cake. The addition of crushed pineapple keeps the cake moist and adds lovely flavor.

CAKE:

- 1   cup all-purpose flour
- 1   teaspoon baking soda
- ½   teaspoon kosher salt
- 1   teaspoon ground cinnamon
- ½   teaspoon grated fresh nutmeg
- 1   cup sugar
- ⅔   cup vegetable oil
- 2   large eggs
- 1½ cups finely grated carrot
- 1   (4-ounce) can crushed pineapple, undrained
- ¼   cup sweetened flaked coconut
- ¼   cup pecans, chopped

Cream Cheese Frosting (recipe follows)

CREAM CHEESE FROSTING:

- 4   ounces cream cheese, softened
- ¼   cup unsalted butter, softened
- ½   teaspoon vanilla extract
- 2½ cups confectioners' sugar

Garnish: chopped pecans

FOR CAKE:

Preheat oven to 350°. Spray a 9-inch cast-iron skillet with cooking spray.

In a large bowl, whisk together flour, baking soda, salt, cinnamon, and nutmeg.

In a medium bowl, whisk together sugar, oil, and eggs. Add sugar mixture to flour mixture, stirring just until combined. Fold in carrot, pineapple, coconut, and pecans. Spread batter into prepared skillet.

Bake until a wooden pick inserted in center comes out clean, 30 to 35 minutes. Let cool completely. Top with Cream Cheese Frosting. Garnish with pecans, if desired.

FOR FROSTING:

In a large bowl, beat cream cheese and butter with a mixer at medium speed until smooth. Beat in vanilla. Gradually add confectioners' sugar, beating until smooth.

STRAWBERRY SKILLET CAKE

When strawberries first come into season, this is my go-to recipe for an easy dessert, because I normally have all the ingredients on hand. I love how the crust gets crispy from the extra sprinkle of sugar on top.

MAKES 1 (9-INCH) CAKE

½ cup unsalted butter, softened
1¼ cups sugar, divided
2 large eggs
½ teaspoon vanilla extract
1⅓ cups all-purpose flour
1¼ teaspoons baking powder
¼ teaspoon kosher salt
½ cup sour cream
1 pound fresh strawberries, stems removed and halved

Preheat oven to 350°. Spray a 9-inch cast-iron skillet with cooking spray.

In a large bowl, beat butter and 1 cup sugar with a mixer at medium speed until fluffy, 3 to 4 minutes, stopping to scrape sides of bowl. Add eggs, one at a time, beating well after each addition. Beat in vanilla.

In a medium bowl, whisk together flour, baking powder, and salt. Reduce mixer speed to low. Gradually add flour mixture to butter mixture alternately with sour cream, beginning and ending with flour mixture, beating just until combined after each addition. Fold in strawberries. Spread batter into prepared skillet. Sprinkle with remaining ¼ cup sugar.

Bake until a wooden pick inserted in center comes out clean, 35 to 40 minutes. Let cool completely on a wire rack.

COCONUT BUTTERMILK POUND CAKE

I can never get enough coconut cake, and this loaf makes getting my fix super-easy.
And don't worry—it can be baked in a regular loaf pan if you don't have a cast-iron version.

MAKES 2 (8½X 4½-INCH) LOAVES

1½ cups unsalted butter, softened
3   cups granulated sugar
5   large eggs, room temperature
3   cups all-purpose flour
2   teaspoons kosher salt
1   teaspoon baking powder
1   cup whole buttermilk
2   teaspoons vanilla extract
1½ cups sweetened flaked coconut,
    toasted and divided
3   cups confectioners' sugar
¼   cup unsweetened coconut milk
1   tablespoon fresh lemon juice

Spray 2 (8½x4½-inch) cast-iron loaf pans with baking spray with flour.

In a large bowl, beat butter with a mixer at medium speed until creamy, about 5 minutes. Add granulated sugar; beat at high speed for 10 minutes, stopping to scrape sides of bowl. Add eggs, one at a time, beating well after each addition.

In a medium bowl, whisk together flour, salt, and baking powder. Reduce mixer speed to low. Gradually add flour mixture to butter mixture, alternately with buttermilk, beginning and ending with flour mixture, beating just until combined after each addition. Beat in vanilla. Stir in 1 cup coconut. Divide batter between prepared pans.

Place in a cold oven. Bake at 300° until a wooden pick inserted in center comes out clean, about 1 hour and 15 minutes. Let cool in pans for 10 minutes. Remove from pans, let cool completely on a wire rack.

In a medium bowl, whisk together confectioners' sugar, coconut milk, and lemon juice. Spread glaze on top of each loaf. Sprinkle with remaining ½ cup coconut.

RASPBERRY-BUTTERMILK COFFEE CAKE

This is the ultimate coffee cake—raspberry jam ribbons swirl throughout the tender buttermilk cake.

MAKES 1 (9-INCH) CAKE

TOPPING:
- ⅓ cup all-purpose flour
- ¼ cup sugar
- ¼ teaspoon kosher salt
- ¼ teaspoon ground cinnamon
- ¼ cup unsalted butter, softened
- ⅓ cup chopped pecans

CAKE:
- ½ cup unsalted butter, softened
- 1 cup sugar
- 2 large eggs
- 1 teaspoon vanilla extract
- 1½ cups all-purpose flour
- 1½ teaspoons baking powder
- ½ teaspoon kosher salt
- ½ cup whole buttermilk
- ½ cup fresh raspberries
- ¾ cup raspberry preserves

GLAZE:
- 1 cup confectioners' sugar
- 1 tablespoon heavy whipping cream

Preheat oven to 350°. Spray a 9-inch cast-iron skillet with cooking spray.

FOR TOPPING:
In a medium bowl, whisk together flour, sugar, salt, and cinnamon. With a mixer at medium speed, beat in butter until crumbly. Stir in pecans; set aside.

FOR CAKE:
In a large bowl, beat butter and sugar with a mixer at medium speed until fluffy, 3 to 4 minutes, stopping to scrape sides of bowl. Add eggs, one at a time, beating well after each addition. Beat in vanilla.

In a medium bowl, whisk together flour, baking powder, and salt. Reduce mixer speed to low. Gradually add flour mixture to butter mixture alternately with buttermilk, beginning and ending with flour mixture, beating just until combined after each addition.

In a small bowl, lightly mash raspberries. Stir in raspberry preserves.

Spread three-fourths of batter into prepared skillet. Spread raspberry mixture onto batter. Top with remaining batter, spreading to edges; sprinkle with topping.

Bake until a wooden pick inserted in center comes out clean, about 50 minutes, loosely covering with foil to prevent excess browning, if necessary.

FOR GLAZE:
In a small bowl, whisk together confectioners' sugar and cream until smooth. Drizzle over cooled cake.

**CLASSIC
TOMATO PIE**
PAGE 77

SUMMER

During the summer, I can never eat enough fresh tomatoes, corn, or blueberries, so I bake with them as often as I can to enjoy all of the season's bright bounty of produce.

POUND CAKE WITH WHIPPED CREAM & BLUEBERRY SAUCE

The beauty of baking in cast iron: evenly distributed heat. This simple pound cake features extra-crunchy edges (just like I like them!) that enclose a tender cake. Trust me, save some for breakfast.

MAKES 2 (8X4-INCH) LOAVES

CAKE:
- 2   cups unsalted butter, softened
- 3   cups sugar
- 4   large eggs
- 4   cups all-purpose flour
- 1½ teaspoons kosher salt
- 1   teaspoon baking powder
- 1⅓ cups whole milk
- 2   teaspoons vanilla extract

BLUEBERRY SAUCE:
- 1   pint fresh blueberries
- 2   tablespoons sugar
- 1   teaspoon lemon zest
- 2   teaspoons cornstarch
- 2   cups water

Sweetened whipped cream, to serve

Preheat oven to 325°. Spray 2 (8x4-inch) cast-iron loaf pans with baking spray with flour.

FOR CAKE:

In a large bowl, beat butter and sugar with a mixer at medium-high speed until fluffy, 3 to 4 minutes, stopping to scrape sides of bowl. Add eggs, one at a time, beating well after each addition.

In a medium bowl, sift together flour, salt, and baking powder. Reduce mixer speed to low. Gradually add flour mixture to butter mixture alternately with milk, beginning and ending with flour mixture, beating just until combined after each addition. Beat in vanilla. Divide batter between prepared pans.

Bake until a wooden pick inserted in center comes out clean, about 1½ hours. Let cool in pans for 10 minutes. Remove from pans, and let cool completely on a wire rack.

FOR SAUCE:

In a small saucepan, combine blueberries, sugar, and zest. In a medium bowl, whisk together cornstarch and 2 cups water until smooth. Add cornstarch mixture to blueberries, and bring to a boil over medium-high heat. Cook until thickened, 2 to 3 minutes. Let cool completely. Serve slices of pound cake with blueberry sauce and whipped cream.

CORN STICKS WITH OKRA

Whether fried, roasted, grilled, or stewed, okra is my summer vegetable of choice.
This corn stick recipe is my new favorite way to enjoy it.

¼   cup butter
1   cup thinly sliced okra
½   cup fresh or thawed frozen
     corn kernels
1½   tablespoons chopped shallot
1½   teaspoons chopped garlic
1   (6-ounce) package cornbread mix
1   (14.5-ounce) can cream-style corn
½   cup whole buttermilk
1   large egg, lightly beaten
3   tablespoons corn oil
¼   teaspoon Cajun seasoning

Preheat oven to 375°. Spray 3 (6-well) cast-iron corn stick pans with cooking spray. Place pans in oven to preheat.

In a medium saucepan, melt butter over medium heat. Add okra, corn kernels, shallot, and garlic; cook, stirring occasionally, until tender, about 8 minutes.

In a medium bowl, stir together cornbread mix, cream-style corn, buttermilk, egg, oil, and Cajun seasoning. Stir in okra mixture. Spoon batter into hot pans, filling wells about ¾ full.

Bake until golden brown, about 30 minutes. Let cool in pans for 10 minutes; serve warm.

BAKING TIP
You can also prepare this recipe in a
9-inch cast-iron skillet, if desired.

BLACKBERRY COBBLER

If you happen upon a blackberry patch and get the opportunity to pick gallons of these jewels,
freeze some so you can bake this cobbler year-round for a cozy reminder of summer.

MAKES 6 TO 8 SERVINGS

6	cups fresh blackberries
1	cup firmly packed light brown sugar
¼	cup fresh orange juice
1	tablespoon vanilla extract
½	teaspoon ground cardamom
¼	cup cornstarch
3	tablespoons water
1½	cups all-purpose flour
¼	cup granulated sugar
1½	teaspoons baking powder
½	teaspoon kosher salt
6	tablespoons cold unsalted butter, cubed
½	cup heavy whipping cream
1	tablespoon sanding sugar

Preheat oven to 375°.

In a 10-inch cast-iron skillet, stir together blackberries, brown sugar, orange juice, vanilla, and cardamom. Cook over medium-high heat, stirring occasionally, until mixture is hot and bubbly, about 10 minutes.

In a small bowl, stir together cornstarch and 3 tablespoons water until smooth. Slowly stir into berry mixture, and cook until thickened, about 3 minutes. Remove from heat.

In a medium bowl, whisk together flour, granulated sugar, baking powder, and salt. Using a pastry blender, cut in cold butter until mixture is crumbly. Stir in cream just until dry ingredients are moistened. Drop dough by 3-inch-round pieces onto berry mixture, and sprinkle with sanding sugar.

Bake until topping is lightly browned, about 30 minutes. Let cool for 30 minutes before serving.

GOOEY BUTTER BISCOFF CAKE

Biscoff—the dreamy cookie butter spread made from my favorite Delta Air Lines in-flight snack—has been on trend in the baking world for some time now. Who doesn't want to dip into a skillet of warm cookie butter cake?

MAKES 1 (10-INCH) CAKE

2 cups heavy whipping cream
1 cup semisweet chocolate morsels
4 ounces cream cheese, softened
6 tablespoons unsalted butter, softened
2 large eggs
1 cup confectioners' sugar
1 cup Biscoff Cookie Spread
¼ teaspoon kosher salt
Garnish: sweetened whipped cream, crushed Biscoff Cookies

Preheat oven to 350°. Spray a 10-inch enamel-coated cast-iron skillet with baking spray with flour.

In a small microwave-safe bowl, microwave cream on medium for 30 seconds. Stir in chocolate until melted and smooth. Pour chocolate mixture into prepared skillet. Refrigerate until firm, about 10 minutes.

In a medium bowl, beat cream cheese and butter with a mixer at medium speed until smooth. Add eggs, confectioners' sugar, cookie spread, and salt, beating until well combined. Spread batter onto chocolate layer in skillet.

Bake until center is almost set, about 40 minutes. Let cool for 10 minutes. Garnish with whipped cream and crushed cookies, if desired. Serve immediately.

APRICOT-ALMOND COBBLER

When warm weather arrives, I keep an eye out for apricots until they finally appear—a gift from the summer fruit gods. This cobbler is always at the top of my to-bake list when I get my hands on this gorgeous fruit.

6   tablespoons unsalted butter
¾   cup all-purpose flour
⅔   cup plus ¼ cup sugar,
     divided
¼   cup almond meal
1   teaspoon baking powder
¼   teaspoon kosher salt
¾   cup whole milk
½   teaspoon almond extract
8   fresh apricots, pitted and halved
¼   teaspoon ground cardamom
Garnish: toasted sliced almonds

Preheat oven to 375°. Place butter in a 10-inch cast-iron skillet, and place in oven until butter is melted.

In a medium bowl, whisk together flour, ⅔ cup sugar, almond meal, baking powder, and salt. Stir in milk and almond extract. Pour flour mixture over melted butter in skillet. (Do not stir.)

In a medium bowl, combine apricots, cardamom, and remaining ¼ cup sugar. Arrange apricots cut side up on top of batter.

Bake until golden brown and a wooden pick inserted in center comes out clean, 40 to 45 minutes. Garnish with almonds, if desired.

BAKING TIP

Canned apricots can be substituted for fresh apricots.

SNICKERDOODLE COOKIE

This childhood favorite cookie—simple and always satisfying—is even better when it's made oversized and baked in cast iron.

MAKES 8 SERVINGS

½ cup unsalted butter, softened
¾ cup plus 1 teaspoon granulated sugar, divided
1 large egg
½ teaspoon vanilla extract
1⅓ cups all-purpose flour
½ teaspoon baking soda
½ teaspoon cream of tartar
¾ teaspoon ground cinnamon, divided
¼ teaspoon kosher salt
½ teaspoon turbinado sugar

Preheat oven to 350°. Spray a 10-inch cast-iron skillet with cooking spray.

In a large bowl, beat butter and ¾ cup granulated sugar with a mixer at medium speed until fluffy, 3 to 4 minutes, stopping to scrape sides of bowl. Add egg and vanilla, beating to combine.

In a medium bowl, whisk together flour, baking soda, cream of tartar, ½ teaspoon cinnamon, and salt. Reduce mixer speed to low. Gradually add flour mixture to butter mixture, beating just until combined. Press dough into bottom of prepared skillet.

In a small bowl, combine turbinado sugar, remaining 1 teaspoon granulated sugar, and remaining ¼ teaspoon cinnamon. Sprinkle over dough.

Bake until set, about 25 minutes.

FARMSTAND CORNBREAD

This is an "everything but the garden hose" kind of recipe. When summer is in full swing,
don't be afraid to bake your cornbread with a variety of vegetables on top.

MAKES ABOUT 8 SERVINGS

2	tablespoons canola oil
2	cups yellow cornmeal
1	cup all-purpose flour
1	tablespoon baking powder
1½	teaspoons kosher salt
2½	cups whole buttermilk
6	tablespoons unsalted butter, melted
2	large eggs
1	cup cubed fontina cheese, divided
⅔	cup sweet corn kernels, divided
1	cup heirloom cherry tomatoes, halved
1	large fresh jalapeño pepper, chopped
¼	cup sliced red onion

Preheat oven to 425°. Pour oil into a 10-inch cast-iron skillet. Place skillet in oven until oil is very hot, about 10 minutes.

In a large bowl, whisk together cornmeal, flour, baking powder, and salt. In a medium bowl, whisk together buttermilk, melted butter, and eggs. Make a well in center of cornmeal mixture; add buttermilk mixture, stirring until combined. Fold in ½ cup cheese and ⅓ cup corn. Carefully pour batter over hot oil in skillet.

Bake for 10 minutes. Remove from oven; top with tomatoes, jalapeño, onion, remaining ½ cup cheese, and remaining ⅓ cup corn. Bake until golden brown and a wooden pick inserted in center comes out clean, about 27 minutes more.

LEMON SHAKER PIE

With just six ingredients including a store-bought piecrust, summer entertaining doesn't get much easier than this pie.

MAKES 1 (9-INCH) PIE

2   **large lemons**
2   **cups plus 2 tablespoons granulated sugar, divided**
1   **(14.1-ounce) package refrigerated piecrusts**
5   **large eggs, divided**
¼   **cup unsalted butter, melted and slightly cooled**
1   **tablespoon water**
Garnish: confectioners' sugar

In a large bowl, zest lemons. Using a sharp knife, remove as much white pith as possible without removing any lemon flesh; discard pith. Wrap lemons in plastic wrap, and freeze for 15 minutes.

Using a mandoline, slice lemons as thin as possible. In bowl with lemon zest, toss together lemon slices and 2 cups granulated sugar until combined. Cover and let stand at room temperature for at least 6 hours or up to 24 hours.

Preheat oven to 425°.

Unroll 1 piecrust, and press into bottom and up sides of a 9-inch cast-iron skillet. In a small bowl, whisk 4 eggs until frothy; whisk in melted butter. Whisk egg mixture into lemon mixture, and pour into prepared crust.

Unroll remaining piecrust, and place on top of lemon mixture. Fold edges under, and crimp as desired. Cut 4 vents in top of dough to release steam. In a small bowl, whisk together 1 tablespoon water and remaining 1 egg. Brush egg mixture over crust. Sprinkle with remaining 2 tablespoons granulated sugar.

Bake for 25 minutes. Reduce oven to 350°. Loosely cover with foil, and bake until golden brown, about 20 minutes more. Let cool completely. Garnish with confectioners' sugar, if desired.

BLUEBERRY-CORNMEAL SKILLET CAKE

This humble skillet cake is for every day...and, yes, you should bake it every day this summer. It's that good.

MAKES 1 (10-INCH) CAKE

1¼ cups all-purpose flour
¾ cup plus 1 tablespoon granulated sugar, divided
⅓ cup yellow cornmeal
1½ teaspoons kosher salt
1 teaspoon baking powder
½ teaspoon baking soda
½ teaspoon lemon zest
1 cup sour cream
9 tablespoons unsalted butter, melted and divided
2 large eggs
1 teaspoon vanilla extract
2 cups fresh blueberries, divided
Garnish: confectioners' sugar

Preheat oven to 350°. Place a 10-inch cast-iron skillet in oven to preheat.

In a large bowl, stir together flour, ¾ cup granulated sugar, cornmeal, salt, baking powder, baking soda, and zest.

In a medium bowl, stir together sour cream, 8 tablespoons melted butter, eggs, and vanilla. Make a well in center of flour mixture. Add sour cream mixture, stirring to combine.

Carefully remove hot skillet from oven. Add remaining 1 tablespoon melted butter, swirling to coat. Add half of batter to pan, spreading in an even layer. Sprinkle 1 cup blueberries over batter. Drop tablespoonfuls of remaining batter over blueberries. Sprinkle with remaining 1 cup blueberries and remaining 1 tablespoon granulated sugar.

Bake until a wooden pick inserted in center comes out clean, about 35 minutes. Let cool on a wire rack for 30 minutes. Garnish with confectioners' sugar, if desired.

CRAB & FRESH CORN PIE

Growing up along the Gulf Coast, my summer days were spent sailing, fishing, and crabbing. When you catch enough fresh blue crabs to fill a bucket, you work extra hard to pick every morsel of sweet meat from their shells. This cornbread recipe is super indulgent with crabmeat baked inside and stirred together with bacon, tomatoes, and fresh corn for a quick topping.

MAKES 6 SERVINGS

CRUST:
- **1** cup all-purpose flour
- **¼** cup yellow cornmeal
- **½** teaspoon kosher salt
- **½** cup cold unsalted butter, cubed
- **5 to 7** tablespoons whole buttermilk

FILLING:
- **1¼** cups heavy whipping cream
- **4** large eggs
- **½** pound lump crabmeat
- **1** cup shredded smoked Gouda cheese
- **¾** cup fresh corn kernels
- **½** teaspoon kosher salt
- **¼** teaspoon ground red pepper
- **¼** teaspoon paprika

TOPPING:
- **¼** pound lump crabmeat
- **2** slices bacon, cooked and crumbled
- **¾** cup quartered cherry tomatoes
- **½** cup fresh corn kernels
- **2** tablespoons chopped green onion
- **2** tablespoons red wine vinegar
- **⅛** teaspoon salt

Preheat oven to 350°.

FOR CRUST:
In a large bowl, whisk together flour, cornmeal, and salt. Using a pastry blender or your fingers, cut in cold butter until mixture is crumbly. Gradually add 5 tablespoons buttermilk, stirring until dry ingredients are moistened. Add remaining 2 tablespoons buttermilk, if needed. Turn out dough onto a lightly floured surface, and shape into a disk. Wrap tightly in plastic wrap, and refrigerate until firm, about 30 minutes.

Let dough stand at room temperature until slightly softened, about 5 minutes. On a lightly floured surface, roll dough into a 12-inch circle. Transfer to an 8-inch cast-iron skillet, pressing into bottom and up sides. Trim excess dough to ½ inch beyond edge of skillet. Fold edges under, and crimp as desired.

FOR FILLING:
In a large bowl, whisk together cream and eggs. Gently stir in crabmeat, cheese, corn, salt, red pepper, and paprika. Pour into prepared crust.

Bake until a knife inserted in center comes out clean, 45 to 50 minutes. Let cool for 30 minutes.

FOR TOPPING:
In a medium bowl, toss together crabmeat, bacon, tomatoes, corn, green onion, vinegar, and salt. Serve with pie.

JALAPEÑO GOAT CHEESE CORNBREAD

If you've ever grown jalapeños in your backyard garden, you know you'll have basketfuls at the end of the summer. Slice them lengthwise and add them to the top of this cornbread for a show-stopping skillet, where the goat cheese and thyme add depth and richness. To tame the heat from the jalapeños, try drizzling your slice with some local honey.

MAKES 1 (12-INCH) SKILLET

5	fresh jalapeños, halved
3	tablespoons canola oil
4	cups cornmeal
2	cups all-purpose flour
½	cup chopped fresh jalapeño
2	tablespoons baking powder
1	tablespoon kosher salt
5	cups whole buttermilk
¾	cup unsalted butter, melted
4	large eggs
2	(4-ounce) packages goat cheese, crumbled
⅓	cup shredded mild Cheddar cheese

Preheat oven to 425°.

Heat a 12-inch cast-iron skillet over medium-high heat. Add halved jalapeños; cook until lightly charred on both sides, about 2 minutes per side. Remove from skillet.

Pour oil into skillet. Place skillet in oven until oil is very hot, about 8 minutes.

In a large bowl, whisk together cornmeal, flour, chopped jalapeño, baking powder, and salt. In another large bowl, whisk together buttermilk, melted butter, and eggs. Make a well in center of dry ingredients; add buttermilk mixture, stirring until combined. Stir in goat cheese. Carefully pour batter over hot oil in skillet. Sprinkle with Cheddar. Top with charred jalapeño, cut side up.

Bake until golden brown and a wooden pick inserted in center comes out clean, about 35 minutes.

RED, WHITE, & BLUE COBBLER

Let this feed-a-crowd cobbler be your centerpiece for summer holidays. You can take it straight from the oven to your picnic table. If you don't have a "big daddy" skillet this size, you can easily split the recipe between two smaller skillets.

MAKES 15 TO 20 SERVINGS

2 **(14.1-ounce) packages refrigerated piecrusts**
5 **pounds fresh strawberries, hulled (about 15 cups)**
6 **cups fresh blueberries**
2 **cups granulated sugar**
½ **cup cornstarch**
3 **tablespoons unsalted butter, cubed**
1 **tablespoon lemon zest**
1 **large egg, lightly beaten**
2 **tablespoons coarse sugar**
Vanilla ice cream, to serve

On a lightly floured surface, unroll 1 piecrust. Brush lightly with water; place another piecrust on top, sealing layers together. Cut 5 (1½-inch-wide) strips, and place on a baking sheet. Refrigerate until ready to use.

Repeat rolling procedure with remaining piecrusts. Using a 3-inch star cutter, cut 5 stars. Using a 2½-inch star cutter, cut 9 stars. Place stars on a baking sheet, and refrigerate until ready to use. Reserve remaining crust for another use.

In a large bowl, stir together strawberries, blueberries, and granulated sugar. Let stand for at least 30 minutes.

Place berry mixture in a 15-inch cast-iron skillet; stir in cornstarch. Cook over medium heat, stirring frequently, until thick and bubbly, about 15 minutes. Remove skillet from heat. Stir in butter and zest.

Preheat oven to 400°.

Place strips on cobbler, cutting to fit, if necessary. Arrange stars on top. Brush dough strips and stars with egg, and sprinkle with coarse sugar.

Bake until crust is golden brown, 25 to 30 minutes. Serve warm with ice cream.

BAKING TIP

Don't have a 15-inch skillet? Prepare this recipe in 2 (9-inch) skillets.

S'MORES BROWNIES

I love to serve these brownies at the end of a dinner party. It's a way to make sure everyone lingers at the table a little longer.

MAKES 8 SERVINGS

1   **(4-ounce) bar unsweetened chocolate, melted**
¾   **cup unsalted butter, melted**
2   **cups sugar**
3   **large eggs**
1½   **teaspoons vanilla extract**
1   **cup all-purpose flour**
¼   **teaspoon kosher salt**
¼   **teaspoon baking powder**
¾   **cup miniature marshmallows**
⅔   **cup chopped graham crackers**
½   **cup semisweet chocolate chunks**
2   **cups large marshmallows**
2   **(4-ounce) bars semisweet chocolate, roughly chopped**
Garnish: chopped graham crackers

Preheat oven to 350°. Spray a 10-inch cast-iron skillet with cooking spray.

In a large bowl, combine melted chocolate and melted butter. Whisk in sugar, eggs, and vanilla until combined.

In a medium bowl, whisk together flour, salt, and baking powder. Stir flour mixture into chocolate mixture. Fold in miniature marshmallows, graham crackers, and chocolate chunks. Spread batter into prepared skillet.

Bake until center is set, 35 to 40 minutes. Remove from oven; top with large marshmallows and chopped chocolate. Bake until marshmallows begin to brown, about 10 minutes more. Garnish with graham crackers, if desired.

PEACH-GINGER COBBLERS

Who doesn't like their own individual skillet of cobbler for dessert? If you don't have mini skillets,
you can bake one large cobbler in a 10-inch skillet.

MAKES 6

½ cup unsalted butter, softened
¼ cup granulated sugar
¾ cup firmly packed light brown
   sugar, divided
1 cup plus 3 tablespoons all-purpose
   flour, divided
½ teaspoon ground nutmeg
¼ teaspoon ground ginger
¼ teaspoon kosher salt
6 to 8 cups fresh peaches, peeled and
   sliced (about 8 medium peaches)
1½ tablespoons grated fresh ginger
1 tablespoon fresh lemon juice
½ teaspoon vanilla extract
½ teaspoon ground cinnamon
1 large egg, lightly beaten
3 tablespoons turbinado sugar

Preheat oven to 375°. Spray 6 (4½-inch) cast-iron skillets with cooking spray.

In a large bowl, beat butter, granulated sugar, and ¼ cup brown sugar with a mixer at medium speed until fluffy, 3 to 4 minutes, stopping to scrape sides of bowl.

In a medium bowl, whisk together 1 cup flour, nutmeg, ground ginger, and salt. Reduce mixer speed to low. Gradually add flour mixture to butter mixture, beating just until combined. Shape dough into a disk. Wrap in plastic wrap, and refrigerate for at least 30 minutes.

In a large bowl, stir together peaches, grated ginger, lemon juice, vanilla, cinnamon, remaining ½ cup brown sugar, and remaining 3 tablespoons flour. Spoon peach mixture into prepared skillets. Place on a baking sheet.

Bake for 15 minutes.

On a lightly floured surface, roll dough to ¼-inch thickness. Using a 3-inch round cutter dipped in flour, cut dough into 6 circles. Top each skillet with a circle. Brush dough with egg, and sprinkle with turbinado sugar.

Bake until tops are golden brown and filling is bubbly, about 30 minutes more.

CHERRY-ALMOND SKILLET CAKE

This cake is reminiscent of a coffee cake but has the tender crumb of an old-fashioned buttermilk cake.

MAKES 1 (10-INCH) CAKE

½   cup unsalted butter, softened
¾   cup sugar
1   large egg
1½   cups all-purpose flour
1   teaspoon baking powder
¼   teaspoon baking soda
¼   teaspoon kosher salt
⅔   cup whole buttermilk
1   cup frozen dark cherries
¼   cup chopped almonds

Preheat oven to 350°.

In a large bowl, beat butter and sugar with a mixer at medium speed until creamy, 3 to 4 minutes, stopping to scrape sides of bowl. Add egg, beating until combined.

In a medium bowl, whisk together flour, baking powder, baking soda, and salt. Reduce mixer speed to low. Gradually add flour mixture to butter mixture alternately with buttermilk, beginning and ending with flour mixture, beating just until combined after each addition. Pour batter into a 10-inch cast-iron skillet. Sprinkle cherries and almonds over batter.

Bake until a wooden pick inserted in center comes out clean, 30 to 35 minutes. Let cool for 20 minutes; serve warm.

CLASSIC TOMATO PIE

This recipe is similar to one my friend Katie and I used to make right out of college, when we lived together and shared our first real kitchen in a 1920s apartment. We both have an affinity for the classic tomato pie, which must—in our humble opinions—include mayonnaise.

MAKES 6 TO 8 SERVINGS

½ (14.1-ounce) package refrigerated piecrusts
2½ pounds assorted heirloom tomatoes, sliced ¼ inch thick and seeded
2 teaspoons kosher salt, divided
1 cup grated Gruyère cheese
1 cup shredded Monterey Jack cheese
¾ cup mayonnaise
1 large egg, lightly beaten
½ cup fresh basil, thinly sliced
1 tablespoon chopped fresh thyme
¼ teaspoon ground black pepper
1 cup chopped red onion
Garnish: fresh basil, chopped fresh thyme

Preheat oven to 425°. Press piecrust into bottom and up sides of a 10-inch cast-iron skillet. Fold edges under, and crimp as desired. Refrigerate for 30 minutes.

Place tomato slices on paper towels; sprinkle with 1 teaspoon salt. Let stand at room temperature for 30 minutes.

In a medium bowl, stir together cheeses, mayonnaise, egg, basil, thyme, pepper, and remaining 1 teaspoon salt. Sprinkle red onion over prepared crust; top with ⅓ of cheese mixture. Layer half of tomatoes in an overlapping pattern; top with ⅓ of cheese mixture. Repeat with remaining tomatoes and remaining cheese mixture.

Bake until golden brown and center is set, 40 to 45 minutes. Let cool completely. Serve at room temperature. Garnish with basil and thyme, if desired.

BAKING TIP
Salting the tomatoes helps draw out extra liquid that could result in a soggy pie.

RASPBERRY-BLACKBERRY SOUR CREAM COBBLER

A sour cream lattice crust cradles summer's finest: raspberries and blackberries. But you can get creative and add any berry combination you have available.

MAKES ABOUT 8 SERVINGS

2 cups all-purpose flour
½ cup plus 1 tablespoon granulated sugar, divided
½ teaspoon salt
1 cup cold unsalted butter, cubed
¾ cup sour cream
2 to 4 tablespoons cold water
4½ cups fresh raspberries
4 cups fresh blackberries
4 tablespoons cornstarch
2 tablespoons fresh lemon juice
1 large egg, lightly beaten
1 tablespoon coarse sugar

In a large bowl, whisk together flour, 1 tablespoon granulated sugar, and salt. Using a pastry blender or your fingers, cut in cold butter until mixture is crumbly. Stir in sour cream. Add water, 1 tablespoon at a time, stirring until a dough forms. (Do not overmix.)

Turn out dough onto a lightly floured surface, and shape into a disk. Wrap in plastic wrap, and refrigerate for at least 30 minutes.

Preheat oven to 350°.

In a large bowl, stir together raspberries, blackberries, cornstarch, lemon juice, and remaining ½ cup granulated sugar. Spoon berry mixture into a 10-inch enamel-coated cast-iron skillet.

On a lightly floured surface, roll dough to ¼-inch thickness. Using a knife or pastry wheel, cut dough into 1¼-inch-wide strips. Arrange strips over filling in a lattice design, trimming excess dough. Brush lattice with egg, and sprinkle with coarse sugar.

Bake until crust is golden brown and filling is bubbly, about 50 minutes. Let cool for 15 minutes before serving.

CLASSIC SOUTHERN CORNBREAD

My grandparents made a skillet of cornbread every day for lunch, and they sat down at the kitchen table around noon for a proper, full meal. Leftover cornbread was saved for supper, and then the last wedge was crumbled into a glass of milk by my grandfather before bed. I love how they savored each slice. I can't pour cornbread batter into a hot skillet without thinking of them.

MAKES 1 (8-INCH, 10-INCH, OR 12-INCH) SKILLET

FOR AN 8-INCH SKILLET:

1	tablespoon canola oil
1	cup cornmeal
½	cup all-purpose flour
1½	teaspoons baking powder
¾	teaspoon kosher salt
1¼	cups whole buttermilk
3	tablespoons unsalted butter, melted
1	large egg

FOR A 10-INCH SKILLET:

2	tablespoons canola oil
2	cups cornmeal
1	cup all-purpose flour
1	tablespoon baking powder
1½	teaspoons kosher salt
2½	cups whole buttermilk
6	tablespoons unsalted butter, melted
2	large eggs

FOR A 12-INCH SKILLET:

3	tablespoons canola oil
4	cups cornmeal
2	cups all-purpose flour
2	tablespoons baking powder
1	tablespoon kosher salt
5	cups whole buttermilk
¾	cup unsalted butter, melted
4	large eggs

FOR AN 8-INCH SKILLET:

Preheat oven to 425°. Pour oil into a deep 8-inch cast-iron skillet. Place skillet in oven until oil is very hot, about 8 minutes.

In a large bowl, whisk together cornmeal, flour, baking powder, and salt. In a small bowl, whisk together buttermilk, melted butter, and egg. Make a well in center of cornmeal mixture; add buttermilk mixture, stirring until combined. Carefully pour batter over hot oil in skillet.

Bake until golden brown and a wooden pick inserted in center comes out clean, about 25 minutes.

FOR A 10-INCH SKILLET:

Follow directions above using a 10-inch skillet; bake until golden brown and a wooden pick inserted in center comes out clean, about 27 minutes.

FOR A 12-INCH SKILLET:

Follow directions above using a 12-inch skillet; bake until golden brown and a wooden pick inserted in center comes out clean, about 35 minutes.

BAKING TIP

The hot oil should shimmer and start to smoke before adding the batter. This helps the center of the cornbread bake evenly and ensure a crisp crust. Use a deep skillet to ensure all of the batter will fit.

**PUMPKIN-
CINNAMON TWIST**
PAGE 97

FALL

Pumpkins and sweet potatoes may take the spotlight during Thanksgiving festivities, but in my kitchen, crisp apples, crunchy pecans, and decadent caramel have a special place in my heart when baking this time of year.

BROWNED BUTTER & PECAN BLONDIES

Blondies have always been one of my favorites, but these are taken over-the-top with cane syrup and lots of pecans.

MAKES 4

BLONDIES:
- ¾ cup unsalted butter
- 1½ cups firmly packed light brown sugar
- 2 large eggs
- 1½ teaspoons vanilla extract
- 1½ cups all-purpose flour
- 2 teaspoons baking powder
- 1 teaspoon salt
- 1 cup pecans, roughly chopped
- ½ cup butterscotch morsels

TOPPING:
- 1 cup cane syrup
- ¼ cup unsalted butter
- ¼ cup heavy whipping cream
- ¼ teaspoon kosher salt
- ½ cup confectioners' sugar
- 2 cups pecan halves

Vanilla ice cream, to serve
Garnish: cane syrup

Preheat oven to 350°. Spray 4 (6-inch) cast-iron skillets with cooking spray.

FOR BLONDIES:
In a medium skillet, melt butter over medium heat. Cook, stirring frequently, until butter turns a medium-brown color and has a nutty aroma, about 10 minutes. Remove from heat, and strain through a fine-mesh sieve.

In a large bowl, beat browned butter and brown sugar with a mixer at medium speed until combined, 1 to 2 minutes. Add eggs, one at a time, beating well after each addition. Beat in vanilla.

In a medium bowl, whisk together flour, baking powder, and salt. Reduce mixer speed to low. Gradually add flour mixture to butter mixture, beating just until combined. Fold in pecans and butterscotch. Divide batter among prepared skillets.

Bake until a wooden pick inserted in center comes out clean, 25 to 27 minutes. Let cool completely.

FOR TOPPING:
In a medium saucepan, bring cane syrup to a boil over medium heat. Boil for 1 minute, stirring frequently. Remove from heat, and stir in butter until melted. Stir in cream and salt. Let cool completely. Whisk in confectioners' sugar; stir in pecans. Pour pecan mixture over cooled blondies. Serve with ice cream, and drizzle with cane syrup, if desired.

ROSEMARY FOCACCIA

Baking focaccia in cast iron yields a crisp bottom, while still keeping the overall texture of the bread soft and pliable.

MAKES 2 (9-INCH) SKILLETS

DOUGH:
- **1** cup warm water (105° to 110°)
- **2** tablespoons sugar
- **1** (0.25-ounce) package active dry yeast
- **2½** cups all-purpose flour
- **1½** teaspoons kosher salt
- **2** tablespoons olive oil

ROSEMARY FOCACCIA:
- **6** tablespoons olive oil, divided
- **Dough (recipe precedes)**
- **4** tablespoons chopped fresh rosemary, divided

Garnish: sea salt, ground black pepper

FOR DOUGH:
In a medium bowl, stir together 1 cup warm water, sugar, and yeast. Let stand until frothy and bubbling, about 5 minutes.

In the bowl of a stand mixer fitted with the paddle attachment, combine flour and salt. With mixer on low speed, add yeast mixture and oil, beating just until combined. Switch to the dough hook attachment. Beat at medium speed until dough is smooth and elastic, about 7 minutes.

Spray a large bowl with cooking spray. Place dough in bowl, turning to grease top. Cover and let rise in a warm, draft-free place (75°) until doubled in size, about 1 hour.

FOR FOCACCIA:
Drizzle 2 tablespoons oil into 2 (9-inch) cast-iron skillets.

Lightly punch down Dough. Add 2 tablespoons rosemary, kneading until combined. Divide dough in half, and place in prepared skillets. Press dough into bottom of skillets. Cover and let rise in a warm, draft-free place (75°) until doubled in size, about 45 minutes.

Preheat oven to 375°.

Using your fingertips, press dough to create divots. Sprinkle with remaining 2 tablespoons rosemary, and drizzle with remaining 2 tablespoons oil.

Bake until golden brown, about 20 minutes. Garnish with sea salt and pepper, if desired.

CARAMEL-PECAN DUTCH BABIES

These puffed little beauties can be served for dessert or a decadent brunch.

CARAMEL SAUCE:

- ⅔ cup sugar
- 3 tablespoons water
- 1 tablespoon light corn syrup
- 1 tablespoon cold unsalted butter
- ¼ cup heavy whipping cream
- ½ teaspoon vanilla extract
- ⅛ teaspoon kosher salt

DUTCH BABIES:

- 6 teaspoons cold unsalted butter
- ½ cup all-purpose flour
- 2 tablespoons sugar
- ½ teaspoon kosher salt
- ⅛ teaspoon ground cinnamon
- ½ cup whole milk
- 1 tablespoon unsalted butter, melted
- 2 large eggs
- Caramel Sauce (recipe preceeds)
- ½ cup toasted pecans, chopped

FOR CARAMEL SAUCE:

In a small saucepan, place sugar. In a small bowl, stir together 3 tablespoons water and corn syrup. Pour over sugar, swirling to combine. Cook over medium-high heat, without stirring, until mixture begins to turn golden brown, about 5 minutes. Remove from heat. Add butter, stirring until melted. (Mixture will foam.)

In a microwave-safe bowl, heat cream until hot but not boiling, about 20 seconds. Add hot cream to caramel, stirring until smooth. Pour into a bowl. Stir in vanilla and salt.

FOR DUTCH BABIES:

Preheat oven to 375°. Place 6 (5-inch) skillets on a large rimmed baking sheet.

Place 1 teaspoon cold butter in each skillet. Place in oven until butter is melted.

In the container of a blender, place flour, sugar, salt, and cinnamon; process until combined. Add milk, melted butter, and eggs; process until smooth, stopping to scrape sides of container. Pour batter over butter in hot skillets.

Bake until puffed and golden brown, about 18 minutes. Serve immediately with Caramel Sauce and pecans.

STICKY LAYER BARS

Butterscotch is always a good idea. Even better, these six-ingredient bars bake in only 20 minutes.

2   sleeves graham crackers (18 graham crackers)
½   cup plus 1 tablespoon unsalted butter, melted
1¼ cups semisweet chocolate morsels
1   cup sweetened flaked coconut
¾   cup butterscotch morsels
½   cup sweetened condensed milk

Preheat oven to 350°. Spray a 10-inch cast-iron skillet with cooking spray.

In the work bowl of a food processor, place graham crackers; pulse until finely ground. Transfer to a medium bowl, and stir in melted butter. Press mixture into prepared skillet.

In a medium bowl, stir together chocolate, coconut, and butterscotch. Sprinkle over graham cracker crust. Pour condensed milk over mixture.

Bake until coconut is lightly toasted, 18 to 20 minutes.

BLACK BOTTOM CRANBERRY-PECAN PIES

I love how the sharp flavor of cranberries is mellowed out when mixed with dark chocolate and pecans.

MAKES 6

1   (14.1-ounce) package refrigerated piecrusts
1   (4-ounce) bar bittersweet chocolate, chopped
2   tablespoons heavy whipping cream
3   large eggs, lightly beaten
1   cup dark corn syrup
⅔   cup sugar
¼   cup unsalted butter, melted
1   teaspoon vanilla extract
2   cups roughly chopped pecans
1   cup fresh cranberries
Sweetened whipped cream, to serve
Garnish: prepared caramel sauce

Unroll piecrusts, and divide into 6 equal portions. Press into bottom and up sides of 6 (5-inch) cast-iron skillets. Fold edges under, and crimp as desired.

In a small saucepan, cook chocolate and cream over medium-heat, stirring frequently, until chocolate is melted and mixture is smooth. Divide chocolate mixture among prepared crusts. Refrigerate for 30 minutes.

Preheat oven to 350°.

In a medium bowl, whisk together eggs, corn syrup, sugar, melted butter, and vanilla until smooth; stir in pecans and cranberries. Pour batter over chocolate mixture in skillets.

Bake until center is set, 30 to 35 minutes. Let cool completely. Serve with whipped cream, and drizzle with caramel, if desired.

BAKING TIP

This recipe can also make 1 (9-inch) pie.
Bake until center is set, 50 minutes to 1 hour.

APPLE-GINGER SCONES

When you bake scones in a wedge pan, there's no need for cutting the dough like most traditional recipes.
Just drop the dough into the wells and bake.

MAKES 16

2   cups self-rising flour
½   cup granulated sugar
1   teaspoon ground ginger
½   teaspoon kosher salt
¼   cup unsalted butter, cubed
1   cup chopped dried apple rings
½   cup plus 2 tablespoons whole
    buttermilk, divided
1   large egg
1   teaspoon vanilla extract
2   tablespoons turbinado sugar

Preheat oven to 400°. Spray 2 (8-well) cast-iron wedge pans with cooking spray.

In a large bowl, whisk together flour, granulated sugar, ginger, and salt. Using a pastry blender or your fingers, cut in butter until mixture is crumbly; stir in apple rings.

In a small bowl, whisk together ½ cup buttermilk, egg, and vanilla. Stir buttermilk mixture into flour mixture just until dry ingredients are moistened.

Divide dough among wells of prepared pans. Dampen fingers with remaining 2 tablespoons buttermilk. Gently pat dough into wells, and sprinkle with turbinado sugar.

Bake until golden brown, about 20 minutes. Let cool in pans for 5 minutes; serve warm.

BAKING TIP
If you don't own a wedge pan, bake in a 9-inch cast-iron skillet and slice into wedges.

PUMPKIN-CINNAMON TWIST

Keep ingredients for this giant cinnamon roll on hand for that first, cool autumn morning.
It will infuse your kitchen with the irresistible smell of pumpkin spice.

MAKES ABOUT 6 SERVINGS

DOUGH:
½ cup warm water (105° to 110°)
½ cup canned pumpkin
2 tablespoons sugar
1½ teaspoons pumpkin pie spice
1 (0.25-ounce) package active
   dry yeast
2½ cups all-purpose flour
1½ teaspoons kosher salt
2 tablespoons unsalted butter,
   melted

FILLING:
½ cup unsalted butter, softened
½ cup firmly packed light brown
   sugar
½ cup finely ground pecans
2 tablespoons ground cinnamon
Pinch kosher salt

GLAZE:
1½ cups confectioners' sugar
¼ cup orange juice

FOR DOUGH:
In a medium bowl, stir together ½ cup warm water, pumpkin, sugar, pumpkin pie spice, and yeast. Let stand until frothy and bubbling, about 5 minutes.

In the bowl of a stand mixer fitted with the paddle attachment, combine flour and salt. With mixer on low speed, add yeast mixture and melted butter, beating just until combined. Switch to the dough hook attachment. Beat at medium speed until dough is smooth and elastic, about 7 minutes.

Spray a large bowl with cooking spray. Place dough in bowl, turning to grease top. Cover and let rise in a warm, draft-free place (75°) until doubled in size, about 1 hour.

Spray a 10-inch cast-iron skillet with cooking spray. Lightly punch down dough. On a lightly floured surface, roll dough into a 16x12-inch rectangle.

FOR FILLING:
Spread butter onto dough. In a small bowl, stir together brown sugar, pecans, cinnamon, and salt. Sprinkle sugar mixture over butter. Starting with one long side, roll dough into a log; pinch seam to seal. Cut in half lengthwise, leaving 2 inches at top intact. Carefully twist dough pieces around each other, making sure cut side stays up. Pinch end together. Carefully spiral dough around itself, and place in prepared skillet. Cover and let rise in a warm, draft-free place (75°) until doubled in size, about 45 minutes.

Preheat oven to 350°.

Bake, uncovered, until golden brown, about 30 minutes. Let cool for 15 minutes.

FOR GLAZE:
In a small bowl, whisk together confectioners' sugar and orange juice until smooth. Drizzle over warm bread. Serve immediately.

CARAMELIZED ONION & PEAR GALETTE

This is the upside-down delight of my dreams... savory and full of caramelized onion slices, pear, thyme, and fontina cheese.

MAKES 1 (10-INCH) SKILLET

CRUST:
- 1¾ cups all-purpose flour
- ½ cup stone-ground yellow cornmeal
- 2 teaspoons sugar
- 1½ teaspoons kosher salt
- ¾ cup plus 1 tablespoon cold unsalted butter, cubed
- ⅓ cup cold water

FILLING:
- ¾ cup unsalted butter
- 8 cups sliced yellow onion (about 1½ pounds)
- 1 teaspoon kosher salt
- ½ teaspoon ground black pepper, divided
- 1 tablespoon sherry
- 1 tablespoon chopped fresh thyme
- 1 Bosc pear, peeled and thinly sliced
- 1 cup grated fontina cheese
- 1 large egg, lightly beaten
- 1 tablespoon stone-ground yellow cornmeal

Garnish: fresh thyme

FOR CRUST:
In the work bowl of a food processor, place flour, cornmeal, sugar, and salt; pulse until combined. Add cold butter, and pulse until mixture is crumbly.

With processor running, add ⅓ cup cold water in a slow, steady stream until a dough is formed. (You may not need all the water.) Shape dough into a disk, and wrap in plastic wrap. Refrigerate for at least 30 minutes.

FOR FILLING:
In a large skillet, melt butter over medium heat. Add onion, salt, and ¼ teaspoon pepper; cook, stirring frequently, until softened and caramelized, about 30 minutes. Add sherry; simmer until evaporated, about 2 minutes. Stir in thyme.

Preheat oven to 375°. Spray a 10-inch cast-iron skillet with cooking spray.

On a lightly floured surface, roll dough into a 12-inch circle. Transfer to prepared skillet, gently pressing dough into bottom (and trimming to edge of skillet). Spread onion mixture onto dough. Layer pears on top of onion mixture, and sprinkle with cheese. Fold edges of dough over filling. Lightly brush with egg. Sprinkle with cornmeal and remaining ¼ teaspoon pepper.

Bake until crust is lightly golden, 35 to 38 minutes. Garnish with thyme, if desired.

APPLE PIE

This classic apple pie is best made with a combination of tart and slightly sweet apples like Granny Smith and Pink Lady. I like to leave the peel on for added color and texture.

MAKES 1 (10-INCH) PIE

THE BEST PIECRUST:
2¾ cups all-purpose flour
2   tablespoons sugar
2   teaspoons kosher salt
1   cup cold unsalted butter, cubed
10 to 14 tablespoons ice water

PIE:
4   pounds apples, cored and sliced
¾   cup granulated sugar
½   cup firmly packed light
     brown sugar
1   teaspoon ground cinnamon
½   teaspoon kosher salt
¼   teaspoon ground ginger
3   tablespoons cornstarch
The Best Piecrust (recipe preceeds)
1   tablespoon heavy whipping cream
1   tablespoon coarse sugar

FOR PIECRUST:
In the work bowl of a food processor, place flour, sugar, and salt; pulse until combined. Add cold butter, and pulse until mixture is crumbly. Add ice water, 1 tablespoon at a time, just until dough comes together.

Divide dough in half, and shape into 2 disks. Wrap tightly in plastic wrap, and refrigerate for at least 2 hours. Dough may be refrigerated for up to 3 days or frozen for up to 2 months.

FOR PIE:
In a large bowl, toss together apples, sugars, cinnamon, salt, and ginger. Let stand for 30 minutes.

Preheat oven to 375°.

Transfer apple mixture to a colander, and drain excess liquid. Place apple mixture back in bowl; stir in cornstarch.

On a lightly floured surface, roll half of The Best Piecrust into a 12-inch circle. Transfer to a 10-inch cast-iron skillet, pressing into bottom and up sides. Fold edges under, and crimp as desired. Spoon apple mixture into prepared crust.

On a lightly floured surface, roll remaining dough to ⅛-inch thickness. Using a sharp knife or a pizza wheel, slice dough into long strips, and place over apple filling in a lattice pattern. Brush dough strips with cream, and sprinkle with coarse sugar. Place skillet on a baking sheet.

Bake for 30 minutes. Reduce oven temperature to 350°, and bake until crust is golden brown and filling is bubbly, about 20 minutes more. Let cool for 1 hour before serving.

BAKING TIPS

Use cold ingredients and combine them quickly to create the perfect flaky piecrust. Combine the apples with sugar and spices for 30 minutes before baking. This helps draw out excess liquid, preventing a runny pie. Be sure to let the pie cool for at least 1 hour before cutting into it to give the filling time to set up.

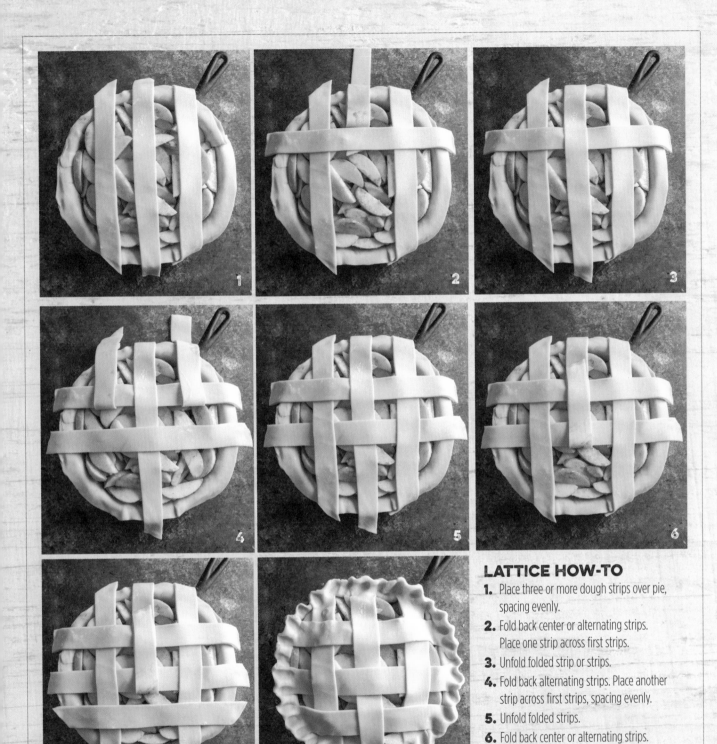

LATTICE HOW-TO

1. Place three or more dough strips over pie, spacing evenly.
2. Fold back center or alternating strips. Place one strip across first strips.
3. Unfold folded strip or strips.
4. Fold back alternating strips. Place another strip across first strips, spacing evenly.
5. Unfold folded strips.
6. Fold back center or alternating strips.
7. Place another strip across first strips, spacing evenly.
8. Unfold folded strips. Crimp as desired.

PECAN-GOAT CHEESE DUTCH BABY

Pecans and goat cheese are a classic Southern pairing and make for a Dutch baby that's both sweet and savory.

3   large eggs, room temperature
½   cup all-purpose flour
½   cup whole milk, room temperature
¼   cup goat cheese
1   tablespoon sugar
1   teaspoon vanilla extract
¼   teaspoon kosher salt
¼   teaspoon ground cinnamon
2   tablespoons unsalted butter, softened
½   cup pecan halves, toasted
Garnish: cane syrup, crumbled goat cheese

Preheat oven to 425°. Place a 10-inch cast-iron skillet in oven to preheat.

In a large bowl, whisk together eggs, flour, milk, goat cheese, sugar, vanilla, salt, and cinnamon until well combined.

Carefully remove hot skillet from oven. Add butter to skillet; let melt. Pour batter over hot butter in skillet.

Bake until puffed and golden brown, 10 to 12 minutes. Top with pecans. Garnish with cane syrup and goat cheese, if desired. Serve immediately.

CORNBREAD WITH SMOKED CHEDDAR & COLLARDS

This cornbread definitely counts toward eating your vegetables. Have another slice.

MAKES 8 TO 10 SERVINGS

2   slices bacon, chopped
1½   cups finely chopped collard greens, firmly packed
2   teaspoons finely chopped fresh sage
2   cups self-rising cornmeal mix
1⅓   cups whole buttermilk
2   large eggs, lightly beaten
3   tablespoons vegetable oil, divided
¼   teaspoon ground black pepper
¾   cup shredded smoked Cheddar cheese

Preheat oven to 425°.

In a 10-inch cast-iron skillet, cook bacon over medium heat until crisp. Remove bacon using a slotted spoon, and let drain on paper towels, reserving drippings in skillet. Add greens and sage; cook until collards are wilted, about 1 minute. Remove from heat.

In a medium bowl, stir together cornmeal mix, buttermilk, eggs, 1 tablespoon oil, and pepper. Stir in collard mixture, bacon, and cheese. Add remaining 2 tablespoons oil to skillet; heat over medium-high heat until hot. Remove from heat. Pour cornmeal mixture over hot oil, smoothing top. (Do not stir.)

Bake until a wooden pick inserted in center comes out clean, about 20 minutes. Let cool in skillet for 10 minutes.

PUMPKIN-MAPLE BREAD PUDDING

This bread pudding quickly warms up cool evenings, and the challah makes for an even richer flavor.

MAKES 8 TO 10 SERVINGS

1   (16-ounce) loaf challah bread,
    cut into 1½-inch cubes
1   cup golden raisins
1¾ cups heavy whipping cream
1⅓ cups canned pumpkin
¾   cup maple syrup
4   large eggs
2   teaspoons pumpkin pie spice
1   teaspoon ground cinnamon
1   teaspoon vanilla extract
⅓   cup pecan halves
Garnish: confectioners' sugar,
    sorghum syrup

Preheat oven to 350°. Spray a 12-inch cast-iron skillet with baking spray with flour.

In a large bowl, stir together bread and raisins. In another large bowl, whisk together cream, pumpkin, maple syrup, eggs, pumpkin pie spice, cinnamon, and vanilla. Pour over bread mixture; stir until combined. Let stand for 20 minutes.

Transfer bread mixture to prepared skillet. Bake until a wooden pick inserted in center comes out clean, 45 to 50 minutes, covering with foil halfway through baking to prevent excess browning, if necessary. Sprinkle with pecans. Garnish with confectioners' sugar and sorghum syrup, if desired.

OATMEAL-TOFFEE COOKIE

Everyone needs a good oatmeal cookie in their repertoire. This one has toffee bits stirred into the dough and a chopped toffee bar sprinkled on top.

1   cup unsalted butter, softened
1½   cups firmly packed light brown
     sugar
2   large eggs
1   teaspoon vanilla extract
1½   cups all-purpose flour
1½   teaspoons baking powder
½   teaspoon kosher salt
1½   cups old-fashioned oats
¾   cup toffee bits
½   cup roughly chopped toffee bar

Preheat oven to 325°. Spray a 12-inch cast-iron skillet with cooking spray.

In a large bowl, beat butter and brown sugar with a mixer at medium speed until fluffy, 3 to 4 minutes, stopping to scrape sides of bowl. Add eggs, one at a time, beating well after each addition. Beat in vanilla.

In a medium bowl, whisk together flour, baking powder, and salt. Reduce mixer speed to low. Gradually add flour mixture to butter mixture, beating just until combined. Stir in oats and toffee bits. Press dough into bottom of prepared skillet. Sprinkle with chopped toffee bar.

Bake until golden brown, 35 to 40 minutes, loosely covering with foil to prevent excess browning, if necessary.

PUMPKIN-PARMESAN BREAD

With sage, pumpkin, ginger, and Parmesan, this loaf tastes like Thanksgiving.

3½ cups all-purpose flour
1⅓ cups sugar
1½ teaspoons kosher salt
1 teaspoon baking soda
1 teaspoon baking powder
1 teaspoon ground ginger
½ teaspoon ground black pepper
5 large eggs, lightly beaten
1¼ cups canola oil
1 (15-ounce) can pumpkin
1 cup grated Parmesan cheese, divided
½ cup chopped fresh sage

Preheat oven to 350°. Spray 2 (8x4-inch) cast-iron loaf pans with baking spray with flour.

In a large bowl, stir together flour, sugar, salt, baking soda, baking powder, ginger, and pepper. Add eggs and oil, stirring well. Stir in pumpkin, ¾ cup Parmesan, and sage. Divide batter between prepared pans. Sprinkle tops with remaining ¼ cup Parmesan.

Bake until a wooden pick inserted in center comes out clean, 1 hour to 1 hour and 5 minutes.

SKILLET APPLE PIE WITH PECAN CRUMBLE

When I make apple crisp or pie, I always save a serving for breakfast the next morning.
It's like a bowl of warm, apple-studded oatmeal...but better.

MAKES 1 (9-INCH) PIE

CRUST:
- 2 cups all-purpose flour
- ¼ cup sugar
- ¼ cup toasted pecans
- ¼ teaspoon kosher salt
- ½ cup cold unsalted butter, cubed
- ⅓ cup heavy whipping cream

FILLING:
- 5 medium Granny Smith apples, peeled, cored, and cut into ⅛-inch-thick slices
- 2 Pink Lady apples, peeled, cored, and cut into ⅛-inch thick slices
- 2 cups sugar, divided
- 1½ tablespoons brandy
- 1 teaspoon vanilla extract
- 2 tablespoons cornstarch
- 2 teaspoons ground cinnamon
- ½ teaspoon ground nutmeg
- ½ teaspoon ground allspice

TOPPING:
- 2⅔ cups all-purpose flour
- ⅔ cup firmly packed light brown sugar
- ½ cup granulated sugar
- ½ cup finely ground toasted pecans
- 2 teaspoons ground cinnamon
- 1 teaspoon kosher salt
- ½ teaspoon ground nutmeg
- 1 cup unsalted butter, melted

Garnish: prepared caramel sauce

FOR CRUST:
In the work bowl of a food processor, place flour, sugar, pecans, and salt; pulse until combined. Add cold butter, and pulse until mixture is crumbly. With processor running, add cream in a slow, steady stream, and process until mixture forms a ball. Shape dough into a disk, and wrap in plastic wrap. Refrigerate for 1 hour.

On a lightly floured surface, roll dough into a 12-inch circle. Press into bottom and up sides of a 9-inch cast-iron skillet. Trim excess dough to ½ inch beyond edge of skillet. Fold edges under, and crimp as desired. Freeze until firm, about 20 minutes.

Preheat oven to 350°. Prick bottom and sides of dough with a fork. Bake for 10 minutes. Leave oven on.

FOR FILLING:
In a large bowl, stir together apples and 1 cup sugar. Let stand for 30 minutes. Strain apples, discarding liquid. Return apples to bowl, and stir in brandy and vanilla.

In a medium bowl, whisk together cornstarch, cinnamon, nutmeg, allspice, and remaining 1 cup sugar. Stir sugar mixture into apples. Pour apple mixture into prepared crust.

FOR TOPPING:
In a medium bowl, whisk together flour, sugars, pecans, cinnamon, salt, and nutmeg. Stir in melted butter until mixture is crumbly. Sprinkle onto apples.

Bake until topping is golden brown and filling is bubbly, 40 to 50 minutes. Let cool for 1 hour before serving. Garnish with caramel sauce, if desired.

BAKING TIP
Gala or Fuji apples are good substitutes if you can't find Pink Lady apples.

SALTED CARAMEL BLONDIES

Not only does homemade salted caramel get swirled into the batter of these blondies,
but a generous pour of caramel tops each one before serving.

BLONDIES:
- ¾ cup unsalted butter, melted
- 1½ cups firmly packed brown sugar
- 3 large eggs
- 2 teaspoons vanilla extract
- 2¼ cups all-purpose flour
- ¾ teaspoon baking powder
- ½ teaspoon kosher salt
- 1⅓ cups pretzels, chopped and divided
- Salted Caramel (recipe follows), divided

SALTED CARAMEL:
- 1 cup sugar
- 2 tablespoons water
- ½ cup heavy whipping cream
- ¼ cup unsalted butter
- 1 teaspoon kosher salt

FOR BLONDIES:
Preheat oven to 350°. Spray a 9-inch cast-iron skillet with cooking spray.

In a large bowl, beat melted butter, brown sugar, and eggs with a mixer at medium speed until combined, 3 to 4 minutes, stopping to scrape sides of bowl. Beat in vanilla.

In a medium bowl, whisk together flour, baking powder, and salt. Reduce mixer speed to low. Gradually add flour mixture to butter mixture, beating until combined. Stir in 1 cup pretzels.

Press half of batter into prepared skillet. Pour ¾ cup Salted Caramel over batter; swirl with a wooden pick. Gently spread remaining batter into skillet. Top with remaining ⅓ cup pretzels.

Bake until a wooden pick inserted in center comes out clean, 25 to 28 minutes, loosely covering with foil to prevent excess browning, if necessary. Drizzle with remaining ¼ cup Salted Caramel.

FOR CARAMEL:
In a large saucepan, sprinkle sugar in an even layer. Add 2 tablespoons water, swirling to combine. Cook over medium-high heat, without stirring, until mixture is amber colored, about 10 minutes. Remove from heat; stir in cream, butter, and salt. Let cool in pan, stirring frequently.

SKILLET PECAN PIE

Don't let making a homemade piecrust scare you—all you need is a food processor and a few ingredients.
The beauty of this rustic pie is that the dough is folded over the filling, so there's no crimping involved.

MAKES 10 TO 12 SERVINGS

CRUST:
3¾ cups all-purpose flour
1 tablespoon sugar
1½ teaspoons kosher salt
1½ cups cold unsalted butter, cubed
¾ cup cold water

FILLING:
½ cup unsalted butter
1 cup firmly packed light brown sugar
½ cup dark corn syrup
⅓ cup cane syrup
1½ teaspoons cornstarch
1½ teaspoons ground cinnamon
1 teaspoon vanilla extract
¼ teaspoon kosher salt
5 large eggs, divided
6 cups pecan halves
1 tablespoon turbinado sugar

Garnish: whipped topping

FOR CRUST:

In the work bowl of a food processor, place flour, sugar, and salt; pulse until combined. Add cold butter, and pulse until mixture is crumbly. With processor running, add ¾ cup cold water in a slow, steady stream until dough comes together but is not sticky (you may not need all of the water). Turn out dough onto a lightly floured surface, and shape into a disk. Wrap in plastic wrap, and refrigerate for at least 30 minutes.

Preheat oven to 375°. Spray a 12-inch cast-iron skillet with cooking spray.

On a lightly floured surface, roll dough into a 15-inch circle. Transfer to prepared skillet, pressing into bottom and up sides.

FOR FILLING:

In a large saucepan, melt butter over medium heat. Add brown sugar, corn syrup, and cane syrup, stirring until sugar is dissolved.

In a small bowl, stir together ½ cup sugar mixture and cornstarch. Return to saucepan. Add cinnamon, vanilla, and salt. Whisk in 4 eggs until combined. Stir in pecans. Pour filling into prepared crust, and gently fold edges of dough over filling. In a small bowl, whisk remaining 1 egg. Brush over crust, and sprinkle with turbinado sugar.

Bake until crust is golden brown and filling is set, about 40 minutes, covering with foil halfway through baking to prevent excess browning, if necessary. Garnish with whipped topping, if desired.

SWEET POTATO PIE

Marshmallows or pecans: that's always the Thanksgiving sweet potato debate. This pie gets
topped with marshmallows, but you can easily add pecans to half of it so everyone gets their holiday favorite.

MAKES 1 (9-INCH) SKILLET

1½ cups graham cracker crumbs
½ cup finely chopped pecans
¾ cup unsalted butter, melted
4 cups cooked mashed sweet
  potatoes (about 4 pounds)
1 cup firmly packed dark brown
  sugar
½ cup heavy whipping cream
3 large eggs, lightly beaten
2 teaspoons lemon zest
1 teaspoon ground cinnamon
¼ teaspoon kosher salt
2 cups miniature marshmallows

Preheat oven to 350°.

In a medium bowl, stir together graham cracker crumbs and pecans.
Add melted butter, stirring until moistened. Using a measuring cup, press
mixture into bottom and up sides of a 9-inch cast-iron skillet.

Bake until golden brown, about 10 minutes. Let cool for 15 minutes.

In a large bowl, stir together sweet potato, brown sugar, cream, eggs, zest,
cinnamon, and salt until well combined. Spoon into prepared crust.

Bake until set, 45 to 55 minutes. Sprinkle with marshmallows, and bake until
browned, about 10 minutes more.

APPLE BUTTER SWEET ROLLS

My grandparents made apple butter every fall and "put it up" to enjoy for months to come. These sweet rolls are smeared with prepared apple butter that you can pick up at your curb market, but the flavor always takes me back to their "utility room"—better known now as a pantry—where jars of apple butter lined the shelves.

MAKES 10

DOUGH:

- 1 cup warm water (105° to 110°)
- 2 tablespoons sugar
- 1 (0.25-ounce) package active dry yeast
- 2½ cups all-purpose flour
- 1½ teaspoons kosher salt
- 2 tablespoons unsalted butter, melted

SWEET ROLLS:

- Dough (recipe precedes)
- ½ cup apple butter
- ½ cup firmly packed light brown sugar
- 2 tablespoons all-purpose flour
- 1 teaspoon ground cinnamon
- 1 Pink Lady apple, thinly sliced
- ¼ cup unsalted butter, softened
- 2 ounces cream cheese, softened
- 2 cups confectioners' sugar
- 2 to 4 tablespoons whole milk
- ¼ teaspoon vanilla extract

FOR DOUGH:

In a medium bowl, stir together 1 cup warm water, sugar, and yeast. Let stand until frothy and bubbling, about 5 minutes.

In the bowl of a stand mixer fitted with the paddle attachment, combine flour and salt. With mixer on low speed, add yeast mixture and melted butter, beating just until combined. Switch to the dough hook attachment. Beat at medium speed until dough is smooth and elastic, about 7 minutes.

Spray a large bowl with cooking spray. Place dough in bowl, turning to grease top. Cover and let rise in a warm, draft-free place (75°) until doubled in size, about 1 hour.

FOR SWEET ROLLS:

Spray a 12-inch cast-iron skillet with cooking spray.

Lightly punch down Dough. On a lightly floured surface, roll dough into a 14x10-inch rectangle. Spread apple butter onto dough.

In a small bowl, stir together brown sugar, flour, and cinnamon. Sprinkle sugar mixture over apple butter; top with apple slices. Starting with one long side, roll dough into a log; pinch seam to seal. Slice into 10 rolls. Place rolls in prepared skillet. Cover and let rise in a warm, draft-free place (75°) until doubled in size, about 45 minutes.

Preheat oven to 350°.

Bake, uncovered, until golden brown, about 30 minutes. Let cool for 15 minutes.

In a medium bowl, beat butter and cream cheese with a mixer at medium speed until smooth. Add confectioners' sugar, milk, and vanilla, beating until smooth. Spread glaze onto warm rolls.

**BROWNED
BUTTER PECAN
ROLLS**
PAGE 136

WINTER

Indulge in the rich flavors of the season. The weather may be blustery, but the kitchen can be a baking haven. Let freshly baked breads and treats give you the comfort you need to share with family and friends.

CHERRY SWEET ROLLS

A quick cherry jam is the centerpiece of these fluffy sweet rolls.

MAKES 12

DOUGH:
- ¼ cup warm water (105° to 110°)
- 2 teaspoons active dry yeast
- ½ cup plus 1 teaspoon sugar, divided
- ½ cup unsalted butter, softened
- 2 teaspoons kosher salt
- 2 large eggs
- 1 cup whole milk
- 1 tablespoon fresh lemon juice
- 4½ cups bread flour

CHERRY FILLING:
- 1 (12-ounce) bag frozen dark sweet cherries, thawed, juice drained and reserved for glaze
- 2 tablespoons sugar
- 1 tablespoon cornstarch
- ⅓ cup cherry preserves

GLAZE:
- 1 cup confectioners' sugar
- 2 tablespoons unsalted butter, melted

ICING:
- 1½ cups confectioners' sugar
- ¼ cup whole milk
- ½ teaspoon vanilla extract

FOR DOUGH:
In a measuring cup, stir together ¼ cup warm water, yeast, and 1 teaspoon sugar; let stand for 5 minutes.

In the bowl of a stand mixer fitted with the paddle attachment, beat butter at medium speed until creamy. Gradually add salt and remaining ½ cup sugar, beating until light and fluffy. Add eggs, milk, and lemon juice, beating until combined. Stir in yeast mixture. Reduce mixer speed to low. Gradually add flour, beating until well combined, about 2 minutes.

Turn out dough onto a lightly floured surface, and knead for 5 minutes. Spray a large bowl with cooking spray. Place dough in bowl, turning to grease top. Cover and let stand in a warm, draft-free place (75°) until doubled in size, about 1½ hours.

FOR CHERRY FILLING:
In a medium saucepan, combine cherries, sugar, and cornstarch. Cook over medium heat, stirring constantly, until bubbly and thickened, 3 to 4 minutes. Remove from heat, and stir in preserves. Let cool completely.

Spray 2 (9-inch) cast-iron skillets with cooking spray.

Lightly punch down dough. On a lightly floured surface, roll dough into a 14x10-inch rectangle. Spread cherry filling onto dough. Starting with one long side, roll up dough, jelly-roll style, and press edge to seal. Slice into 12 rolls, and place in prepared skillets. Cover and let stand in a warm, draft-free place (75°) until doubled in size, about 45 minutes.

Preheat oven to 350°. Bake, uncovered, until golden brown, about 30 minutes. Let cool in pans for 5 minutes.

FOR GLAZE:
In a small bowl, whisk together confectioners' sugar, 3 tablespoons reserved drained cherry juice, and melted butter. Brush over hot rolls. Let cool for 30 minutes.

FOR ICING:
In a medium bowl, whisk together confectioners' sugar, milk, and vanilla until smooth; drizzle over rolls.

ONION TWIST BREAD

Caramelized onions, roasted garlic, and cheese fill this savory masterpiece.

MAKES 6 TO 8 SERVINGS

DOUGH:
- ¼ cup warm water (105° to 110°)
- 2 teaspoons active dry yeast
- 3 cups bread flour
- ¼ cup sugar
- 2 teaspoons kosher salt
- ¼ cup unsalted butter, softened
- 1 cup whole milk
- 1 large egg

FILLING:
- 1 head garlic
- 2 tablespoons olive oil
- 1 large yellow onion, chopped
- ½ cup grated Parmesan cheese
- ¼ cup unsalted butter, softened
- 2 tablespoons fresh thyme leaves

FOR DOUGH:
In a medium bowl, stir together ¼ cup warm water and yeast; let stand for 5 minutes.

In a large bowl, stir together flour, sugar, and salt. In the bowl of a stand mixer fitted with the paddle attachment, beat butter at medium speed until creamy. Add yeast mixture and ¼ of flour mixture, beating until smooth. Add ¼ of flour mixture, milk, and egg; beat until smooth. Add remaining flour mixture, and beat until smooth.

Turn out dough onto a lightly floured surface, and knead 10 to 12 times. Spray a large bowl with cooking spray. Place dough in bowl, turning to grease top. Cover and let stand in a warm, draft-free place (75°) until doubled in size, 1½ hours to 2 hours.

FOR FILLING:
Preheat oven to 400°. Cut ¼ inch off top of garlic, and wrap garlic in foil. Bake until soft, about 1 hour. Let cool completely. Press garlic head, and remove roasted garlic; set aside.

In a medium skillet, heat oil over medium heat. Add onion; cook, stirring occasionally, until onion is caramel colored, 20 to 25 minutes. Let cool completely.

In the work bowl of a food processor, combine cooked onion, roasted garlic paste, cheese, butter, and thyme. Process until mixture forms a smooth, thick paste, 2 to 3 minutes.

Spray a 10-inch cast-iron skillet with cooking spray.

On a heavily floured surface, roll dough into a 14x10-inch rectangle. Spread onion filling onto dough, leaving a 1-inch border on long sides. Starting with one long side, roll up dough, jelly-roll style, and press edge to seal. Using a sharp knife, cut roll in half lengthwise. Carefully twist dough pieces around each other, and form into a circle. Using a cake lifter, place dough in prepared skillet. Cover and let stand in a warm, draft-free place (75°) until doubled in size, about 1 hour.

Preheat oven to 350°. Bake for 30 minutes. Cover with foil, and bake until a wooden pick inserted in center comes out clean, about 40 minutes more. Serve warm.

CHOCOLATE POUND CAKES

There's nothing more humble and comforting than a pound cake—especially one with chocolate.

¼ cup unsweetened cocoa powder
¼ cup boiling water
1 cup unsalted butter
⅔ cup plus 2 tablespoons granulated sugar, divided
⅔ cup firmly packed light brown sugar
3 large eggs
1⅔ cups all-purpose flour
1 teaspoon baking powder
½ teaspoon kosher salt
2 ounces semisweet chocolate, melted and cooled
1½ teaspoons vanilla extract
½ teaspoon almond extract
2 cups quartered fresh strawberries
1 teaspoon fresh lemon juice
Sweetened whipped cream, to serve

Preheat oven to 350°. Spray 6 (5-inch) cast-iron skillets with baking spray with flour. Place on a large rimmed baking sheet.

In a small bowl, whisk together cocoa and ¼ cup boiling water until smooth. Let cool to room temperature.

In a large bowl, beat butter, ⅔ cup granulated sugar, and brown sugar with a mixer at medium speed until fluffy, 3 to 4 minutes, stopping to scrape sides of bowl. Add eggs, one at a time, beating well after each addition.

In a medium bowl, whisk together flour, baking powder, and salt. Reduce mixer speed to low. Gradually add flour mixture and cocoa mixture to butter mixture, beating just until combined. Beat in melted chocolate and extracts. Spoon batter into prepared skillets, smoothing tops.

Bake until a wooden pick inserted in center comes out clean, about 23 minutes. Let cool completely on a wire rack.

In a medium bowl, stir together strawberries, lemon juice, and remaining 2 tablespoons granulated sugar. Let stand for 30 minutes. Serve pound cakes with whipped cream and strawberries.

BANANAS FOSTER BREAD PUDDING

I love a classic bourbon bread pudding, but the brandy really punches up the flavor
and gives a nod to one of my favorite cities, New Orleans.

MAKES 6 SERVINGS

BREAD PUDDING:
- 2½ cups whole milk
- ⅔ cup firmly packed light brown sugar
- ⅓ cup granulated sugar
- 2 tablespoons brandy
- 2 tablespoons unsalted butter, melted
- 1 teaspoon vanilla extract
- ¼ teaspoon kosher salt
- ¼ teaspoon ground nutmeg
- ¼ teaspoon ground cinnamon
- 4 large eggs
- 1 (12-ounce) loaf day-old French bread, cut into 1-inch cubes
- Banana-Brandy Sauce (recipe follows)
- Garnish: ground cinnamon

BANANA-BRANDY SAUCE:
- ½ cup firmly packed light brown sugar
- ½ cup water
- 3 tablespoons brandy
- 2 tablespoons unsalted butter
- ⅛ teaspoon kosher salt
- 2 medium bananas, sliced

FOR BREAD PUDDING:
In a large bowl, whisk together milk, sugars, brandy, melted butter, vanilla, salt, nutmeg, cinnamon, and eggs. Add bread cubes, pressing with a spoon. Cover and refrigerate for 4 hours.

Preheat oven to 350°. Spray 6 (5-inch) cast-iron skillets with baking spray with flour. Place on a large rimmed baking sheet. Divide bread mixture among prepared skillets.

Bake until puffed and golden brown, about 25 minutes. Serve warm with Banana-Brandy Sauce. Garnish with cinnamon, if desired.

FOR SAUCE:
In a medium skillet, combine brown sugar, ½ cup water, brandy, butter, and salt over medium heat, stirring occasionally. Reduce heat to medium-low; simmer for 5 minutes. Stir in bananas; cook until warmed, about 2 minutes. Serve immediately.

CHEDDAR & ONION YEAST ROLLS

A pan of these yeast rolls is like a hug from your grandmother.

MAKES 13

4   tablespoons vegetable oil, divided
1   cup minced onion
1½ cups warm whole milk (105°
    to 110°), divided
1   (0.25-ounce) package active
    dry yeast
4   teaspoons sugar, divided
1   large egg, lightly beaten
1   cup shredded sharp Cheddar
    cheese
1   teaspoon kosher salt
4¾ cups bread flour
½   cup freshly grated Parmesan
    cheese

In a 12-inch cast-iron skillet, heat 2 tablespoons oil over medium heat. Add onion; cook, stirring frequently, until tender, about 5 minutes. Remove from heat, and let cool completely.

In a small bowl, stir together ½ cup warm milk, yeast, and 1 teaspoon sugar. Let stand until mixture is foamy, about 5 minutes.

In a large bowl, stir together egg, Cheddar, salt, cooked onion, yeast mixture, remaining sugar, remaining 1 cup warm milk, and remaining 2 tablespoons oil. Gradually stir in flour until a soft dough forms.

Turn out dough onto a lightly floured surface, and knead until smooth and elastic, about 5 minutes. Spray a large bowl with cooking spray. Place dough in bowl, turning to grease top. Cover and let stand in a warm, draft-free place (75°) until doubled in size, about 1 hour.

Punch dough down. Cover and let stand for 10 minutes.

Divide dough into 13 portions, and roll each portion into a ball. Spray same cast-iron skillet with cooking spray, and place dough balls in skillet. Cover and let stand in a warm, draft-free place (75°) until doubled in size, about 1 hour.

Preheat oven to 350°. Sprinkle dough with Parmesan. Bake until golden brown, 15 to 20 minutes, loosely covering with foil to prevent excess browning, if necessary. Serve warm.

BROWNED BUTTER PECAN ROLLS

Filled with browned butter and chopped pecans, these sweet rolls get drenched in
cane syrup instead of the familiar cream cheese frosting.

ROLLS

3½ cups all-purpose flour, divided
1 (0.25-ounce) package active
  dry yeast
½ cup whole milk
½ cup sour cream
⅓ cup unsalted butter, cubed
⅓ cup sugar
1 teaspoon kosher salt
1 large egg, lightly beaten
1 teaspoon vanilla extract
Browned Butter Filling (recipe follows)
1 cup pecans, toasted and chopped
½ cup cane syrup

BROWNED BUTTER FILLING

½ cup unsalted butter
½ cup sugar
1 teaspoon salt
1 teaspoon ground cinnamon

FOR ROLLS:

In the bowl of a stand mixer fitted with the dough hook attachment, combine 1½ cups flour and yeast.

In a medium saucepan, combine milk, sour cream, butter, sugar, and salt. Cook over medium heat, stirring occasionally, until mixture registers 120° on a candy thermometer. With mixer on low speed, add milk mixture to flour mixture, beating until combined. Add egg and vanilla; beat until combined. Increase mixer speed to medium. Gradually add remaining 2 cups flour, beating until dough is smooth and elastic, about 5 minutes. (Dough should pull away from sides of bowl but stick to bottom.)

Spray a large bowl with cooking spray. Place dough in bowl, turning to grease top. Cover and let rise in a warm, draft-free place (75°) until doubled in size, about 1 hour and 15 minutes.

Spray a 10-inch cast-iron skillet with cooking spray. Lightly punch down dough. Cover and let stand for 5 minutes.

On a lightly floured surface, roll dough into a 14x10-inch rectangle. Spread Browned Butter Filling onto dough; sprinkle with pecans. Starting with one long side, roll dough into a log; pinch seam to seal. Slice into 12 rolls. Place rolls in prepared skillet. Cover and let rise in a warm, draft-free place (75°) until doubled in size, about 45 minutes.

Preheat oven to 350°. Bake, uncovered, until golden brown, about 30 minutes. Let cool in pan for 30 minutes. Drizzle with cane syrup.

FOR FILLING:

In a medium saucepan, melt butter over medium heat. Cook, stirring occasionally, until butter turns a medium-brown color and has a nutty aroma, about 8 minutes. Remove from heat, and let cool to room temperature. Refrigerate until slightly hardened but spreadable, about 30 minutes.
In a large bowl, beat browned butter, sugar, salt, and cinnamon with a mixer at medium speed until light and fluffy. Cover and refrigerate for up to 1 week.

CRANBERRY-PEAR CRUMBLE BARS

If you've never thought about baking bars in cast iron, give it a try. You'll love how crispy the bottoms get.

MAKES 9

CRUMBLE:

- 1⅔ cups all-purpose flour
- ¾ cup old-fashioned oats
- ⅓ cup firmly packed light brown sugar
- ⅓ cup granulated sugar
- ¾ teaspoon baking powder
- ½ teaspoon kosher salt
- ¾ cup plus 2 tablespoons unsalted butter, softened

FILLING:

- 2 cups fresh or frozen cranberries
- ½ cup granulated sugar
- 3 tablespoons unsalted butter
- ¼ cup firmly packed light brown sugar
- 7 cups chopped peeled Bosc pears, cut into ½-inch cubes
- ½ teaspoon ground cinnamon
- ½ teaspoon ground cardamom
- ¼ cup cornstarch

Preheat oven to 375°. Spray a 10-inch square cast-iron skillet with baking spray with flour.

FOR CRUMBLE:
In a large bowl, combine flour, oats, sugars, baking powder, and salt. Stir in butter until mixture is crumbly. Press ⅔ of mixture into bottom of prepared skillet. Reserve remaining crumble mixture.

FOR FILLING:
In a medium bowl, toss together cranberries and granulated sugar. Set aside.

In a large saucepan, melt butter over medium heat. Whisk in brown sugar. Stir in pears, cinnamon, and cardamom; cook until tender, about 20 minutes.

Drain excess liquid; crush half of pears with a potato masher. Stir in cranberry mixture and cornstarch. Spoon over prepared crust, and sprinkle with reserved crumble mixture.

Bake until fruit is bubbly and crumble is golden brown, about 50 minutes.

UPSIDE-DOWN MONKEY BREAD

No canned biscuits in this monkey bread recipe! And the extra effort is completely worth it.

DOUGH:

1   cup warm water (105° to 110°)
2   tablespoons sugar
1   (0.25-ounce) package active dry yeast
2½ cups all-purpose flour
1½ teaspoons kosher salt
2   tablespoons unsalted butter, melted

MONKEY BREAD:

½   cup unsalted butter
¾   cup firmly packed light brown sugar
3   tablespoons hot coffee
½   cup plus 2 tablespoons chopped pecans, divided
½   cup granulated sugar
1   tablespoon ground cinnamon
Dough (recipe precedes)

FOR DOUGH:

In a medium bowl, stir together 1 cup warm water, sugar, and yeast. Let stand until frothy and bubbling, about 5 minutes.

In the bowl of a stand mixer fitted with the paddle attachment, combine flour and salt. With mixer on low speed, add yeast mixture and melted butter, beating just until combined. Switch to the dough hook attachment. Beat at medium speed until dough is smooth and elastic, about 7 minutes.

Spray a large bowl with cooking spray. Place dough in bowl, turning to grease top. Cover and let rise in a warm, draft-free place (75°) until doubled in size, about 1 hour.

Preheat oven to 350°.

FOR MONKEY BREAD:

In a 10-inch cast-iron skillet, melt butter over medium heat. Add brown sugar and coffee; bring to a boil. Cook, stirring frequently, until sugar is dissolved, about 3 minutes. Remove from heat. Sprinkle with ½ cup pecans.

In a large resealable plastic bag, combine granulated sugar and cinnamon.

Lightly punch down dough; shape dough into 2-inch balls. Working in batches, place dough balls in plastic bag. Shake until coated with sugar mixture. Arrange dough over butter mixture in skillet. Sprinkle with remaining 2 tablespoons pecans.

Bake until golden brown, about 30 minutes. Let cool in pan for 2 minutes. Invert onto a serving platter or tray. Serve immediately.

CARAMELIZED ONION CORNBREAD

Not only does this cornbread have caramelized onion rings, but bacon and cheese, too.
Serve it with a bowl of chili, or make it a meal by itself.

5	slices thick-cut bacon
⅓	cup minced yellow onion
2	tablespoons vegetable oil
1	large Vidalia onion, sliced ¼ inch thick
2	cups stone-ground yellow cornmeal
1	cup all-purpose flour
1	tablespoon baking powder
1½	teaspoons kosher salt
¼	teaspoon onion powder
½	cup shredded sharp Cheddar cheese
2½	cups whole buttermilk
6	tablespoons unsalted butter, melted
2	large eggs

Preheat oven to 425°.

In a 10-inch cast-iron skillet, cook bacon over medium heat until crisp, about 8 minutes. Remove bacon, and let drain on paper towels, reserving drippings in skillet. Add minced onion to skillet; cook until tender, about 4 minutes. Remove from skillet.

Wipe skillet clean, and heat oil over medium heat. Place onion slices in oil, filling bottom of skillet to edges. Cook onions until tender and golden brown, about 8 minutes. Remove from heat. Roughly chop cooled bacon.

In a large bowl, whisk together cornmeal, flour, baking powder, salt, and onion powder. Stir in cheese. In a medium bowl, whisk together buttermilk, melted butter, and eggs. Make a well in center of dry ingredients. Add buttermilk mixture, stirring until combined. Fold in bacon and minced onion. Carefully pour batter over sliced onion in skillet.

Bake until golden brown and a wooden pick inserted in center comes out clean, about 27 minutes. Let cool in skillet for 10 minutes. Invert onto a wire rack, and let cool completely.

PARKER HOUSE SKILLET ROLLS

I love making these rolls on Christmas Day and timing them to come out of the oven when family arrives.
No one can resist popping the buttery pockets into their mouth. If they make it to the dinner table, they are
perfect when filled with beef tenderloin and horseradish sauce.

MAKES ABOUT 48

1½ cups whole milk, divided
¼ cup sugar
2 teaspoons active dry yeast
4 to 4½ cups all-purpose flour, divided
6 tablespoons unsalted butter, melted, plus more for brushing
2 large eggs
1 tablespoon kosher salt
½ cup plus 1 teaspoon unsalted butter, softened and cut into 48 cubes

In a small bowl, whisk together ½ cup milk, sugar, and yeast. Let stand until mixture is foamy, about 10 minutes. Stir ½ cup flour into yeast mixture.

In the bowl of a stand mixer fitted with the dough hook attachment, beat melted butter, eggs, and remaining 1 cup milk at low speed until combined. Add yeast mixture, beating to combine. Add 1 cup flour and salt; beat to combine. Gradually add remaining flour, 1 cup at a time, beating until dough comes together and begins to pull away from sides of bowl, 2 to 3 minutes. (Dough will be sticky but not unmanageable. If dough is too sticky, add more flour, ¼ cup at a time, until it comes together.)

Spray a large bowl with cooking spray. Place dough in bowl, turning to grease top. Cover and let stand in a warm, draft-free place (75°) until doubled in size, 2 to 2½ hours.

On a lightly floured surface, turn out dough. Divide dough in half, and gently shape each half into a ball. Cover and let rest for 10 minutes.

Spray 2 (12-inch) cast-iron skillets with cooking spray. Roll half of dough into a 14x12-inch rectangle, about ¼ inch thick. Using a 2½-inch round cutter, cut dough, rerolling scraps as necessary. Repeat with remaining dough.

Brush each circle with melted butter, and place one cube of softened butter on bottom half of each one. Fold circles over, and press to seal. Place in prepared skillets. Cover and let stand in a warm, draft-free place (75°) until puffed, about 30 minutes.

Preheat oven to 350°. Brush rolls with melted butter. Bake until golden brown, 20 to 25 minutes. Brush with additional melted butter.

PINEAPPLE-CURRY UPSIDE-DOWN CAKE

Always one of my favorite desserts—for its caramelized pineapple top and perfectly crumbly cake—this pineapple upside-down cake gets amped up with madras curry powder and ground ginger.

MAKES 1 (10-INCH) CAKE

1   (3-ounce) package candied ginger, finely chopped
¾   cup unsalted butter, divided
⅓   cup honey, divided
½   teaspoon madras curry
½   fresh pineapple, cored and sliced
1   cup sugar
2   large eggs
2   cups all-purpose flour
2   teaspoons baking powder
½   cup whole milk
½   teaspoon vanilla extract

Preheat oven to 350°.

In a 10-inch cast-iron skillet, cook ginger, ½ cup butter, and 3 tablespoons honey over medium heat for 5 minutes, stirring constantly. Transfer mixture to a large bowl, reserving 2 tablespoons mixture in skillet.

Add curry, remaining 2⅓ tablespoons honey, and remaining ¼ cup butter to skillet; cook until bubbly. Remove from heat; place pineapple in a fan around skillet.

To ginger mixture, add sugar, and beat with a mixer at medium speed until fluffy. Add eggs, one at a time, beating well after each addition.

In a medium bowl, whisk together flour and baking powder. Reduce mixer speed to low. Gradually add flour mixture to ginger mixture alternately with milk, beginning and ending with flour mixture, beating just until combined after each addition. Stir in vanilla. Spoon over pineapple, using a spatula to smooth batter to edges of skillet.

Bake until a wooden pick inserted in center comes out clean, 28 to 30 minutes. Let cool in pan for 10 minutes. Invert cake onto a serving plate. Drizzle with remaining syrup from pan, and serve warm.

DUTCH OVEN BREAD

Save this recipe for January when you need a cold-weather weekend baking project.
Everyone will be impressed with your baking skills.

DUTCH OVEN BREAD:
4½ cups all-purpose flour
1 tablespoon kosher salt
½ teaspoon active dry yeast
2¼ cups lukewarm water
⅓ cup yellow cornmeal, divided

FOR DUTCH OVEN BREAD:
In a large bowl, stir together flour, salt, and yeast. Add 2¼ cups lukewarm water, and stir with hands until a sticky dough forms. Cover bowl with plastic wrap or a kitchen towel; let rise at room temperature overnight or up to 24 hours.

On a lightly floured surface, pat dough into a circular shape. Fold four edges in toward center; turn dough smooth side up. Sprinkle with flour, and cover with plastic wrap. Let rise at room temperature for 2 hours.

Place a 4- to 6-quart cast-iron Dutch oven in cold oven. Preheat oven to 500°. Sprinkle top of dough generously with cornmeal. Using a large spatula, turn dough over; sprinkle with remaining cornmeal.

Place dough in preheated Dutch oven. (Use a wooden spoon to gently push dough into bottom of pan, if necessary.) Cover and bake for 30 minutes. Uncover and bake 15 to 20 minutes more. Let cool completely on a wire rack.

FOR MULTI-GRAIN TOPPED BREAD:
Prepare dough, and let rise as directed. Stir together **3 tablespoons raw sunflower seeds, 1 tablespoon rolled oats, 1 tablespoon dried minced onion, 1 tablespoon wheat bran, 2 teaspoons coarse sea salt, 1 teaspoon poppy seeds, 1 teaspoon sesame seeds, and 1 teaspoon flax seed**. Sprinkle over bread dough (instead of cornmeal) before baking.

FOR CRANBERRY-PECAN BREAD:
In the first step, stir together **3 cups all-purpose flour, 1½ cups whole-wheat flour, salt, and yeast. Stir in 1 cup dried cranberries, 1 cup chopped pecans, and 1½ teaspoons ground cinnamon**; continue as directed.

FOR ROSEMARY-CHEESE BREAD:
In the first step, stir **1 cup grated Gruyère cheese, 1 tablespoon chopped fresh rosemary, and 1 teaspoon ground black pepper** into flour mixture. Continue as directed. After first 30 minutes of baking, sprinkle bread with **¼ cup grated Gruyère**.

BREAD BAKING TIPS

MEASURING MATTERS

Using a knife, stir the flour around to fluff it up. Use a measuring cup to scoop the flour, then level off the cup using the flat edge of a knife.

TEST YOUR YEAST

Combine warm water, yeast, and sugar, and wait 5 minutes until frothy and bubbling. If the mixture doesn't froth or bubble, chances are your yeast has expired and you will need to try a new package. Use a fresh package of yeast for the best results. (Tip: 1 (0.25-ounce) package yeast = 2¼ teaspoons yeast)

KNEAD TO KNOW

Once the dough comes together, you will need to knead it until it's smooth and elastic. This develops the gluten, which gives the bread good structure and a nice chewy texture.

- By hand: 10 minutes
- With a stand mixer: 7 minutes

CRUST PERFECTION

Using an egg wash before baking bread gives the crust a glossy finish.
To make an egg wash, beat 1 large egg with 1 tablespoon water until frothy. If you want to sprinkle seeds, wheat, or oats over the loaf before baking, brush the loaf with egg wash first to make sure the toppings adhere. Finally, misting or brushing cold water over the loaf before baking can help crisp up the crust.

PEANUT BUTTER-CHOCOLATE CHIP SKILLET COOKIE

This is my ultimate cookie, with melted peanut butter, chocolate chips, and a crunchy oatmeal top.

MAKES ABOUT 4 SERVINGS

½ cup unsalted butter, softened
¾ cup firmly packed light brown sugar
1 large egg
1 teaspoon vanilla extract
¾ cup all-purpose flour
¾ teaspoon baking powder
¼ teaspoon kosher salt
¾ cup old-fashioned oats, divided
½ cup creamy peanut butter
⅓ cup semisweet chocolate morsels

Preheat oven to 325°. Spray a 7-inch cast-iron skillet with cooking spray.

In a large bowl, beat butter and brown sugar with a mixer at medium speed until fluffy, 3 to 4 minutes, stopping to scrape sides of bowl. Add egg and vanilla; beat until combined.

In a medium bowl, whisk together flour, baking powder, and salt. Reduce mixer speed to low. Gradually add flour mixture to butter mixture, beating just until combined. Stir in ½ cup oats.

Press half of dough into bottom of prepared skillet; spread peanut butter onto dough. Drop tablespoonfuls of remaining dough over peanut butter. Sprinkle with chocolate and remaining ¼ cup oats.

Bake until lightly browned, about 45 minutes, loosely covering with foil to prevent excess browning, if necessary. Let cool for 15 minutes.

BROWNED BUTTER-THYME CORNBREAD

Dog-ear this recipe for when you want your cornbread to be a little extra-special.
Fresh thyme-infused browned butter quickly elevates this family favorite.

MAKES 1 (12-INCH) SKILLET

¾ cup unsalted butter
10 sprigs fresh thyme
3 tablespoons canola oil
4 cups cornmeal
2 cups all-purpose flour
¼ cup fresh thyme leaves
2 tablespoons baking powder
1 tablespoon kosher salt
1 tablespoon ground black pepper
4 cups whole buttermilk
4 large eggs
⅔ cup honey
Honey and butter, to serve

Preheat oven to 400°.

In a 12-inch cast-iron skillet, melt butter over medium heat. Add thyme sprigs; cook until butter turns a medium-brown color and has a nutty aroma, 3 to 4 minutes. Pour butter into a medium bowl; discard thyme. Wipe skillet clean.

Add oil to skillet. Place skillet in oven until oil is very hot, about 8 minutes.

In a large bowl, whisk together cornmeal, flour, thyme leaves, baking powder, salt, and pepper. Add buttermilk, eggs, and honey to browned butter in medium bowl; whisk until combined. Make a well in center of dry ingredients; add buttermilk mixture, stirring until combined. Carefully pour batter into hot oil in skillet.

Bake until golden brown and a wooden pick inserted in center comes out clean, 35 to 40 minutes. Serve with honey and butter, if desired.

BAKING TIP
To keep the crust crispy, carefully turn the cornbread out of the skillet as soon as possible. Letting it cool in the skillet steams the crust.

EASY APPLE-BUTTERMILK COBBLER

Each fall, my husband's parents pick heirloom apples in North Carolina and share their bounty with us. This rustic, stir-together cobbler is an easy way to thank them.

MAKES 8 SERVINGS

½   cup unsalted butter, cubed
1   cup all-purpose flour
⅔   cup granulated sugar
⅓   cup firmly packed light brown sugar
1½ teaspoons baking powder
½   teaspoon kosher salt
1   cup whole buttermilk
1   teaspoon vanilla extract
¼   teaspoon almond extract
3   cups sliced Gala apple
1   teaspoon ground cinnamon
Garnish: confectioners' sugar

Preheat oven to 350°. Place butter in a 10-inch cast-iron skillet. Place skillet in oven until butter is melted.

In a medium bowl, whisk together flour, granulated sugar, brown sugar, baking powder, and salt. Stir in buttermilk and extracts. Pour flour mixture over melted butter in skillet.

In a medium bowl, toss together apple and cinnamon; scatter over flour mixture.

Bake until lightly browned, 30 to 35 minutes. Garnish with confectioners' sugar, if desired.

RUM RAISIN COFFEE CAKE

Rum-soaked raisins stud this streusel-topped cake that can be eaten any time of day.

MAKES 1 (10-INCH) CAKE

RAISIN MIXTURE:
½ cup spiced rum, warmed
½ cup raisins
½ cup golden raisins
⅓ cup firmly packed light brown sugar

TOPPING:
½ cup all-purpose flour
¼ cup firmly packed light brown sugar
1 teaspoon ground cinnamon
¼ teaspoon kosher salt
¼ cup unsalted butter, softened
⅓ cup walnuts, chopped

CAKE:
1 cup unsalted butter, softened
1½ cups granulated sugar
½ cup firmly packed light brown sugar
2 large eggs
1 cup sour cream
1½ teaspoons vanilla extract
1 teaspoon spiced rum, room temperature
2 cups all-purpose flour
1 teaspoon baking powder
¼ teaspoon kosher salt
¼ cup golden raisins

GLAZE:
1½ cups confectioners' sugar
1½ tablespoons whole milk
1½ tablespoons aged rum

FOR RAISIN MIXTURE:
In a small bowl, stir together warm rum, raisins, and golden raisins. Cover and let stand for 30 minutes. Drain, and reserve 2 teaspoons liquid. Stir reserved 2 teaspoons liquid and brown sugar into raisins. Set aside.

Preheat oven to 350°. Spray a 10-inch cast-iron skillet with cooking spray.

FOR TOPPING:
In a medium bowl, whisk together flour, brown sugar, cinnamon, and salt. With a mixer at medium speed, beat in butter until crumbly. Stir in walnuts; set aside.

FOR CAKE:
In a large bowl, beat butter and sugars with a mixer at medium speed until fluffy, 3 to 4 minutes, stopping to scrape sides of bowl. Add eggs, one at a time, beating well after each addition. Beat in sour cream, vanilla, and rum.

In a medium bowl, whisk together flour, baking powder, and salt. Reduce mixer speed to low. Gradually add flour mixture to butter mixture, beating just until combined. Spread half of batter into prepared skillet. Sprinkle with raisin mixture, and top with remaining batter. Sprinkle with topping.

Bake until a wooden pick inserted in center comes out clean, 65 to 70 minutes, loosely covering with foil to prevent excess browning, if necessary. Sprinkle with golden raisins.

FOR GLAZE:
In a small bowl, whisk together confectioners' sugar, milk, and rum. Drizzle over cooled cake.

CHEESY GARLIC ROLLS

Sure, you can serve these with a bowl of soup...but it'll be hard to keep yourself from eating the entire pan right when they come out of the oven.

MAKES ABOUT 20

1 (16-ounce) bag deli pizza dough
1 (8-ounce) container mozzarella pearls
¼ cup unsalted butter, melted
1 tablespoon finely chopped fresh parsley
1 teaspoon Italian seasoning
1 teaspoon garlic powder
½ teaspoon kosher salt

Preheat oven to 400°. Spray a 10-inch cast-iron skillet with cooking spray.

On a lightly floured surface, roll dough to ½-inch thickness. Using a 2-inch round cutter, cut dough, rerolling scraps as necessary. In center of each dough circle, place 4 mozzarella pearls. Wrap dough around cheese, and seal. Place in prepared skillet, seam side down.

Bake until golden brown, about 20 minutes.

In a small bowl, stir together melted butter, parsley, Italian seasoning, garlic powder, and salt. Brush rolls with seasoned butter mixture. Serve immediately.

BAKING TIP

If you can't find mozzarella pearls, cut fresh mozzarella into 1-inch pieces.

INDEX